THE SUICIDE MACHINE

DETROIT FREE PRESS STAFF

The writers: Patricia Anstett, Ariana E. Cha, Kirk Cheyfitz, Chris Christoff, David Crumm, Brian Dickerson, Sheryl James, Georgea Kovanis, Antoinette Martin, Kate McKee, David Migoya, Lori Montgomery, Neal Rubin and Wendy Wendland

Project editor: Ron Dzwonkowski
Copy editing: Alexander B. Cruden, Deborah Leiderman
Art direction and cover design: Kris Belden
Graphics: Martha A. Thierry
Design/production: Katharine P. Bagdon, Betty Bazemore, Kris Belden, David Dombrowski
Photo editing: Todd Winge
Photo production: Kathryn Trudeau
Cover photo: Stephen R. Nickerson

Research librarians: Andrew Bailey, Shelley Lavey, Alice Pepper, Chris Schmuckal and Victoria Turk

Printed in the United States of America on recycled paper.

Detroit Free Press Inc. 1997
321 W. Lafayette Blvd.
Detroit, Michigan 48226

ISBN 0-937247-73-1

CONTENTS

PART THREE: THE PEOPLE

PART FOUR: THE ASSISTED SUICIDE DEBATE

PART FIVE: EDITORIAL

FOREWORD

By Heath Meriwether, Publisher, Detroit Free Press

"Who's Kevorkian?" asked 8-year-old Amy Kiska of her reporter-mother, Pat Anstett.

"He's a person who helps people die," Anstett answered. "He either puts a gas mask on your face or he gives you a blood shot," a term Amy uses to describe any intravenous procedure.

"Ohhh, that doesn't sound very good — I would like to die in my sleep, just like Nana," Amy said, remembering her grandmother's gentle death from cancer.

"You know, Amy, that's what much of this debate is all about," Anstett concluded. "It's about making sure that doctors and patients understand people can die in their sleep, without suffering, just like Nana."

This conversation between loved ones mirrors the ones we hope occur all over the nation, following Detroit Free Press coverage of the issues as presented in this book, in which Anstett's reporting has played an important role.

For a long time at the Free Press, we've felt the need to step back from the daily headlines about Dr. Jack Kevorkian, and try to make sense of what has been one of the most significant stories of our time: the debate over physician-assisted suicide and death with dignity.

That debate too often has been diverted by the questionable practices of the man called "Doctor Death" and the in-your-face antics of his lawyer, Geoffrey Fieger. By taking a detailed look at Kevorkian's own written guidelines on assisted suicide, and then applying them to the cases of 47 people he helped die, we felt we could help people see the larger picture.

What we found almost seems contradictory, but suggests why we felt this in-depth look was so significant: Kevorkian doesn't even follow his own proposed guidelines. Yet for many of his patients, he was the best doctor they ever saw.

"At the end of the day, what Kevorkian did was force medicine to confront its own shortcomings," said Brian Dickerson of the Free Press, who wrote and edited several major stories included in this book.

This book raises questions we hope readers across the country will force policy makers to answer:

Is this the way we want this issue to be handled in a caring, civilized society? Does medicine need to rethink how it treats the dying, when people become so desperate they must resort to Dr. Kevorkian?

INTRODUCTION

Hero to some, horror to others, Dr. Jack Kevorkian forced the debate over assisted suicide upon an entire society simply by doing it, again and again and again.

While helping at least 47 people die, Kevorkian scoffed at the law, scorned elected and religious leaders and won over juries.

In March 1997, as Kevorkian faced new crimnal charges, the U.S. Supreme Court pondered assisted suicide and the Michigan Legislature once again tried to stop it from happening, the Free Press presented an extraordinary look at the people who made Jack Kevorkian famous.

A team of reporters spent six months examining the lives of the people who came to Kevorkian to die. They found:

— Kevorkian's practices showed no consistent standards in deciding whom to help die, when to help them, or whether someone is competent to choose suicide.

— Many who died with Kevorkian's help sought him out after other doctors or medical institutions failed to provide care that might have made their lives tolerable. For some, he seemed to offer a chance to regain control of their lives, even if only to end them.

— Although only a few friends and relatives of the dead criticize Kevorkian's methods, his secrecy and frugality sometimes deprived people of the dignity they sought in death.

— The aftermath of a Kevorkian-assisted suicide can be more painful and traumatic for loved ones than the aftermath of a conventional suicide, or even a natural death.

This book explores these and related issues and tells the dramatic story of Kevorkian's seven-year odyssey as witnessed by people who were there, including the dead. Hundreds of interviews, recordings, official records and personal documents show how this suicide machine worked in Michigan since 1990.

In addition to what was a six-day series March 3-8, 1997, in the Free Press, this book includes the newspaper's first report on Jack Kevorkian, before his name became synonymous with suicide. Readers also will find in-depth profiles of Kevorkian, his flamboyant lawyer, and a physician some call the good Dr. Death; examinations of alternatives to assisted suicide and related issues, and the historical context of Kevorkian's 1915 predecessor.

The argument over assisted suicide will scream for resolution before the great baby boom wave of the U.S. population reaches its terminal years in the first decades of the new century.

But already, it is a deadly serious issue. Jack Kevorkian and 47 people have seen to that.

— *Ron Dzwonkowski*

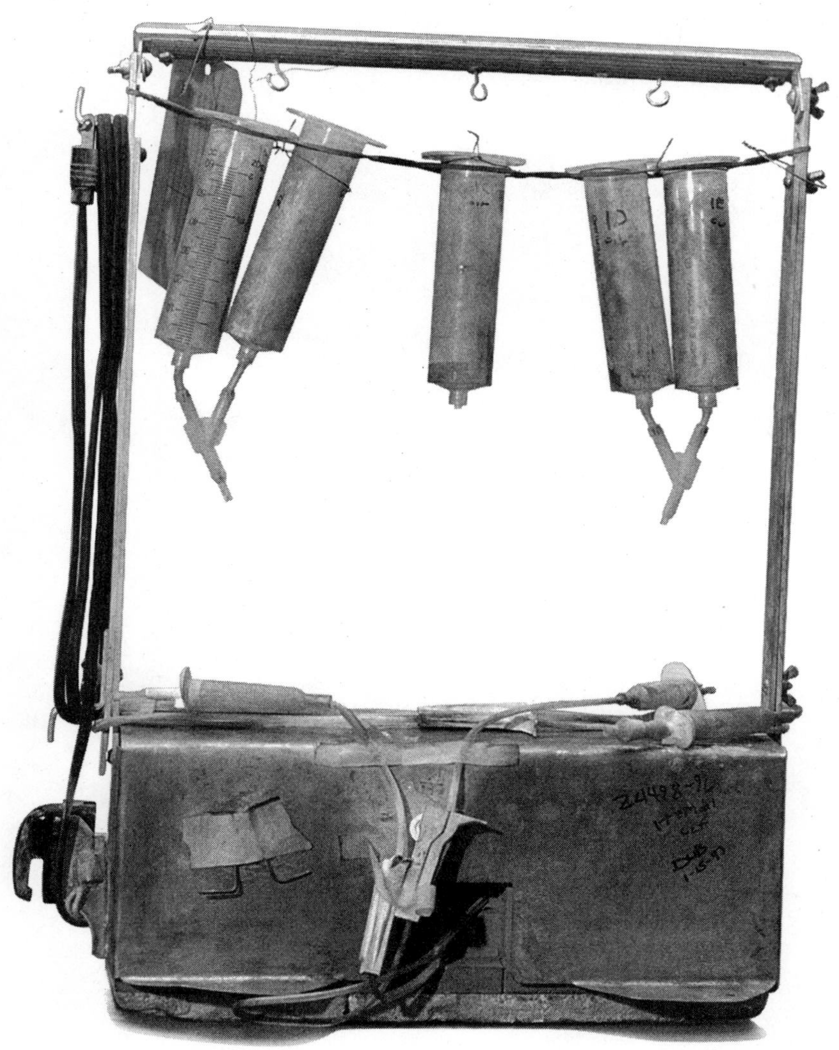

SPECIAL TO THE FREE PRESS

One version of a Kevorkian machine for assisting suicide.

PART ONE:

THE 47 LIVES

DEATH EXPRESS

SUMMER OF '96

Shirley Cline was in a hurry.

Divorced, disinherited and devastated by yet another recurrence of the cancer she had battled for four years, she phoned a right-to-die organization not far from her home in Oceanside, Calif., near San Diego.

"Do you have Jack Kevorkian's telephone number?" she asked. "I want his help to die."

The volunteer who answered the phone, a clinical social worker, listened sympathetically as Cline detailed the operations that had failed to restore her health. When she described the abdominal pain that kept her up nights, the volunteer suggested a pain specialist at Cline's HMO, Kaiser Permanente.

But Cline, 63, was no longer interested in temporary relief. She didn't call the specialist.

A few days later the right-to-die volunteer E-mailed a summary of Cline's case to Janet Good, an activist for the cause in Michigan, who screened entreaties for Kevorkian.

If Cline had called a few months earlier, she might have waited a while for an appointment with Kevorkian.

Though defiant as ever in his rhetoric, Dr. Death had moved cautiously in the 2½ years since his 1993 release from jail following a hunger strike.

He had attended just one suicide in all of 1994, and only seven more in the next 17 months as he awaited trial for four earlier deaths.

But now it was the summer of 1996, and Jack Kevorkian was making up for lost time.

In May, jurors had acquitted him of criminal charges for the third time in as many trials. His most persistent nemesis, Oakland County Prosecutor Richard Thompson, was fighting for his political life. And two federal appeals courts had ruled that state laws prohibiting assisted suicide might be unconstitutional.

A triumphant Kevorkian vowed that never again would the law come between him and suffering people who wanted to die.

By summer's end, Kevorkian would preside over the deaths of 13 other people — more in three months than his total for the previous three years.

Most of those 13 died within 24 hours of meeting him.

But even by the standards of that fast-paced summer, Shirley Cline's death came with extraordinary speed.

On July 4, just a week after calling in response to the E-mail, Kevorkian met her in a Bloomfield Township motel room.

Scarcely three hours later, as her dazed son and two friends looked on, Cline was dead, Kevorkian's fourth suicide in less than a month.

Twelve days before Cline's June 21 call for Kevorkian, Ruth Neuman, 69, a recently widowed diabetic, checked out of a New Jersey nursing home and flew to Michigan.

Kevorkian's lawyer, Geoffrey Fieger, told reporters that Kevorkian had been counseling Neuman for several months, and that she had "been incapacitated many years." That didn't jibe with neighbors' descriptions of a popular mah-jongg and canasta player who'd moved into a Columbus, N.J., retirement village with her husband in 1993.

What's clear is that Neuman, still grieving over her husband's death in November, was newly traumatized by a stroke that had left her partially paralyzed. She was hospitalized in New Jersey on May 22, transferred to the nursing home on June 5 — and died in Michigan five days later.

Nine days after that, in the gathering dusk of a Tuesday evening, an anxious Ralph Jones pushed a wheelchair through the automatic doors of North Oakland Medical Center.

Slumped in the seat was the still-warm body of his wife, Lona, a 58-year-old mother of two who had died with Kevorkian's help an hour or so earlier.

Lona Jones, a nurse who lived with her husband in Chester, Va., had undergone surgery for removal of a benign brain tumor at Duke University Medical Center in Durham, N.C. When the tumor recurred, instead of enduring another operation, she and Ralph headed north to Michigan — and Kevorkian.

In the emergency room, Jones said only that he and his wife had been driving in the neighborhood when she stopped breathing.

But the high concentration of carbon monoxide in her bloodstream suggested Kevorkian's involvement. So did the vaguely familiar middle-aged man who, ever so courteously, asked the nurse whether he might have Lona Jones' wheelchair back.

Sorry, said the nurse, who figured police would want to look at it.

At his home in Culver City, near Los Angeles, Dennis Garling put down the telephone and replayed his conversation with his mother, Shirley Cline.

Was she serious? Was she really planning to spend the Fourth of July in Michigan with Jack Kevorkian?

Garling knew his mother was losing her four-year battle with bowel cancer. He knew she was in pain and that her digestive system rebelled at most of the medicine doctors prescribed to allay her discomfort.

And he knew that she felt humiliated by the ileostomy bag she'd worn to collect her body's waste since her most recent surgery. No matter that Garling, her only son, had used a similar appliance for 30 years; for Cline, who was so meticulous about her appearance, the bag was a fetid reminder of her body's betrayal.

But Kevorkian? Had it really come to that?

Garling could scarcely believe it. Just two weeks ago, his mother and a boyfriend, Bob Barrows, had gone dancing.

Still, he knew better than to argue with her. So when he called her back, he asked if he could go along.

"It just doesn't seem appropriate to say good-bye at the airport," Garling told her.

Shirley Cline spent her last day in California as she had spent so many that year — in intractable pain. But there was no time for self-pity as she threw herself into frenzied preparations for death.

Dwight Smith, a pastor of the Unitarian congregation Cline had joined after being diagnosed with cancer, helped her plan a memorial service for July 13.

He recalled Cline mentioning as an aside her delight with the performance of a stock she'd bought.

"It had doubled and doubled and doubled. And she was so pleased," Smith recalled. "I mean, this is the day before. She knows what she's going to do. I know what she's going to do. And she got a big charge out of the fact that she could have found and bought that stock."

Cline had always taken delight in her investment prowess, especially after being cut out of her mother's multimillion-dollar will.

Later that day, Cline's younger brother, John Green, estranged from her since their mother's death, came over.

Cline moved from bed to chair and back again, lying first on her side, then on her stomach, never quite managing to get comfortable.

Garling and Green kept pace with her agitated orbit, following her from the living room to her bedroom and back as she dispensed instructions about the disposition of her estate and her body.

Cline did not want to delay her trip to Michigan. She worried that commercial airlines would soon deem her too sick to fly.

Green kissed his sister good-bye about 11 p.m. Cline and Garling tried to sleep. Neither succeeded.

They wound up talking until 5 a.m.

Outside, the sky was beginning to brighten. Dawn was coming.
Independence Day.

The nonstop flight from San Diego was grueling for Cline, her son and the two close friends who came along. But they had little time to relax once they reached their motel.

Kevorkian arrived around 8 p.m., with Good and Neal Nicol, a hospital-supplies salesman who frequently assisted him.

There was a short counseling session — the first and last face-to-face meeting of Kevorkian and Cline — with Cline holding fast to her decision to die.

Then, while Kevorkian and Nicol mixed drugs and fussed over Kevorkian's suicide machine, Good drew Garling aside and made an unusual request.

Since Michigan had suspended Kevorkian's license to practice medicine, she explained, the doctor had a problem obtaining drugs for his work. The Seconal that would lull Cline to sleep, for instance, came from one of Kevorkian's previous assisted suicides.

Was there any Seconal in his mother's medicine cabinet back home? she asked. Any other narcotics? And, if so, could Garling please mail them when he got home?

Garling looked at Good blankly. Even in the emotional turmoil of his mother's impending death, he registered that he was being asked to participate in a felony. Excuse me? he thought. You want me to send Kevorkian narcotics through the mail?

But Garling didn't want to rock the boat — not now, with his mother so close to the deliverance she sought.

"Sure," he told Good. "I'll send them just as soon as I get home."

Across the room, Kevorkian and Nicol had inserted an intravenous line into Cline's arm and begun to tell her how to use the suicide machine.

"When you are ready," Nicol said, showing her a string release to start the drugs flowing, "all you need to do is pull …"

But Cline had already pulled.

Nicol looked surprised. He had been about to tell her that she could still change her mind.

But Cline was writing her own script now, and it was time to fade to black.

"Well, Shirley, if you have any second thoughts," Nicol continued feebly. "… Well, it's a little late now."

Around midnight, her body was left at William Beaumont Hospital in Royal Oak.

Neuman ... Jones ... Cline ... As the days broadened into midsummer, the Kevorkian death roll lengthened.

... Rebecca Badger ... Elizabeth Mercz ... Louise Siebens ...

At the time, none of the deaths seemed remarkable. Bette Lou Hamilton had been crippled. Neuman, too. Jones and Cline had cancer; Mercz and Siebens had Lou Gehrig's disease. And Rebecca Badger had MS.

Or did she?

In an autopsy, Oakland County Medical Examiner L.J. Dragovic found no evidence of the disease. But with Kevorkian suicides occurring so regularly, the results were widely ignored as more bickering between Oakland County authorities and Fieger.

Only weeks later, when Badger's own physician retracted her MS diagnosis, did the possibility sink in that Kevorkian may have made a mistake.

But it was Judith Curren's death that vaulted Kevorkian back to the front page.

Curren had made a June 4 suicide appointment, but overslept and missed her flight to Detroit. Kevorkian agreed to schedule a second try for Aug. 15.

At 42, Curren was among the youngest to die with Kevorkian, although she had been incapacitated longer than many of her predecessors. Curren had Chronic Fatigue Syndrome — a poorly understood illness that some physicians dismissed as a neurosis.

So when police in her Massachusetts hometown revealed that Curren had filed a series of domestic-abuse complaints against her husband, a psychiatrist, reporters and investigators swarmed with renewed zeal, speculating that Kevorkian had been a pawn in a murder plot.

That theory foundered as evidence accumulated that Franklin Curren had spent most of the previous two years fighting, rather than encouraging, his wife's fitful march toward self-destruction.

But as the rumors receded, Kevorkian was coming under renewed scrutiny. Many who had sympathized when Kevorkian was on trial wondered whether he had grown careless after his third acquittal. Kevorkian had made a point, they said, but he was getting sloppy.

In fact, Kevorkian was operating pretty much as he always had, as a creature of impulse. His first assisted suicide, the 1990 death of Janet Adkins, raised questions at least as troubling as those posed by the recent deaths of Badger or Curren.

And his ad hoc arrangements for obtaining drugs and transporting corpses recalled his earliest days in Royal Oak, when he'd gone door to door in search of a suicide venue.

Keith Howarth, owner of Noir Leather, an ostentatiously kinky purveyor of erotic clothing and sexual props on Washington Avenue, remembers a day in the spring of 1990 when the slight, silver-haired Kevorkian, who lived in an apartment up the block, stopped to chat.

As Howarth listened raptly, Kevorkian described his still-untested "Mercitron" suicide machine and his vision of a future with state-supported "medicide clinics."

For now, Kevorkian said, he needed a place to plug in his equipment. Was Noir Leather available?

Howarth, a publicity-savvy entrepreneur whose racy, display-window fashion shows had aroused controversy, was intrigued. Impishly, he upped the ante: Would Kevorkian consider staging his first assisted suicide in Noir Leather's window?

Kevorkian demurred. Besides electricity, he explained, he required privacy. His own van, a rusted 1968 Volkswagen, might fit the bill, if he could find a suitable power source, he said.

A few days later, Howarth told Kevorkian his lawyer had vetoed the idea of making Noir Leather or its electricity available.

But he'd given some thought to Kevorkian's problem.

"How about a public park?" Howarth said. "Don't they have electrical hookups?"

— *Brian Dickerson*

The Beginning

JUNE 1990-DECEMBER 1992

Long before most people ever heard of Dr. Jack Kevorkian, Marjorie Wantz suspected he might be the doctor she had dreamed of.

It was spring 1990 and Kevorkian, a 61-year-old pathologist who'd been unemployed for most of the last decade, was trolling Oakland County in search of a site for his first assisted suicide.

He knew he was about to make history, but hardly anyone was paying attention. Most people still dismissed his jerry-built suicide machine as a Rube Goldberg curiosity. Most newspapers were unwilling to print his ads soliciting patients for "special death counseling."

Wantz had heard of Kevorkian, though. And he had her full attention.

Wantz, a 57-year-old west Michigan woman plagued by mysterious pelvic pain, had all but given up on doctors. That May, as Kevorkian looked for a place to try out the device he called the Mercitron, the former teacher's aide and her husband were suing Lane Mercer, one of the dozen or so doctors who'd treated her in the previous three years.

None of Wantz's doctors had been able to explain or relieve the "constant burning, pulling, throbbing, stuck feeling" in her vagina, but Wantz was certain Mercer had caused it.

Mercer, a gynecologist at the University of Chicago Hospitals, had performed laser surgery to remove some precancerous growths on Wantz's genitals in 1988. Her suit charged that he had "used the wrong laser," leaving her with third-degree burns.

Wantz looked forward to a generous settlement, and promised to buy her eldest son a new house with the money.

In the meantime, she had her pain to reckon with.

Wantz was pretty sure laser burns were only part of the problem. When an electronic scan in spring 1991 showed a surgical "needle tip" may have been left in her tissue during a prior operation, she focused on that, calling it a "hook."

But the hook was never recovered, and, if it existed at all, Wantz's subsequent doctors dismissed it as an explanation for her symptoms.

Wantz told her priest that none of her doctors was any good. With each passing month, she became more convinced that only Kevorkian could help.

Janet Adkins was a vigorous, 54-year-old college instructor from Portland, Ore., who wanted to die. Kevorkian, not yet a household name, wanted to help.

From his telephone conversations with her husband, Kevorkian knew Adkins was in no physical pain and that her Alzheimer's disease was in its early stages. Adkins' psychiatrist insisted she had years of useful life ahead and assured Kevorkian she was "the wrong person for a test case" of his suicide machine.

But Adkins wanted to be dead before Alzheimer's seriously affected her life.

On Monday morning, June 4, 1990, in a quiet public park, as Adkins reclined on a bed in the back of Kevorkian's Volkswagen van, he hooked her up to the suicide machine and showed her how to throw the switch that would send deadly chemicals to stop her heart.

Ten minutes later, certain she was dead, he called the Oakland County Medical Examiner's Office and tried to explain what a "doctor-assisted suicide" was.

The arriving investigator found a somewhat shaken Kevorkian wiping his hands. Nervous, unpracticed and not much good at finding a vein to start an intravenous line, Kevorkian had stuck Adkins with a needle five times before successfully starting the IV. Her blood still stained his hands and pants.

But Kevorkian's sense of occasion soon overcame his post-mortem butterflies, and he began talking excitedly of the historic event he had just orchestrated. He was endlessly helpful to the authorities, answering every question they asked. He acknowledged that he had met Adkins only two days before he helped her die and that he had interviewed her formally only once.

He said he had decided to stage Adkins' suicide in the park — "and in my own old van, despite the indignity" — only after being turned down by virtually everyone else.

In the Oakland County Prosecutor's Office, no one was sure what the official response should be.

Four days after Adkins' death, Prosecutor Richard Thompson sought a civil injunction barring Kevorkian from using his suicide machine. He followed up with a murder indictment.

Thompson seemed to have covered all the legal bases, but events would soon bear out Kevorkian's boast that the courts were irrelevant; neither civil injunctions nor the threat of criminal prosecution could stop him.

The more enduring consequence of Thompson's two-front legal assault was to bring two important people into Kevorkian's fold.

Geoffrey Fieger was a flamboyantly successful malpractice lawyer whose showmanship and talent for dramatizing the suffering of sick people would transform the Kevorkian crusade.

Sherry Miller, a 42-year-old Roseville woman who had divorced her husband and relinquished custody of her two children since contracting multiple sclerosis 12 years earlier, appeared as a defense witness in the civil proceedings against Kevorkian. She said she wanted to follow in Adkins' footsteps, and would soon get her wish, injunction or no injunction.

While Kevorkian was making history, Wantz was still blazing a desperate trail from one specialist to another. Along the way, she read a magazine article about Kevorkian, and called him to suggest she might be just the sort of patient he was seeking.

Kevorkian encouraged her to try more painkillers and stay in touch.

So Wantz continued her odyssey, going from Detroit's Sinai Hospital to the Mayo Clinic in Minnesota to the Cleveland Clinic and back to Sinai, even though she and her husband were forced to sell their home to pay mounting medical bills.

She underwent 10 surgeries; none relieved her pain.

Mildred Gast, the woman in the next trailer at the Meadow Stream mobile home park near Benton Harbor, often had to keep her air conditioner on all night to drown out her neighbor's loud moans.

Doctors couldn't explain the pain. Many urged Wantz to seek psychiatric help, and one even tried to have Wantz involuntarily committed to a mental hospital.

Dr. John Finn, medical director of Hospice of Michigan, was apparently the last pain specialist to consult on Wantz's case. He prescribed powerful drugs, including synthetic morphine. None worked.

Finn couldn't explain the pain and wasn't convinced it was organic, but he took Wantz's talk of suicide seriously, noting in her file in the summer of 1991: "I am very much concerned … about her psychological condition."

The Rev. Eugene Sears was worried, too. He had officiated at Wantz's wedding in late 1986. She seldom attended his church in St. Joseph after that, but on several occasions, at Wantz's request, Sears drove out to her trailer in nearby Sodus to dispense communion and read the gospel at her bedside.

"I always had a little difficulty in understanding how much of her pain was real and how much of it — how can I say it? I guess the word 'hypochondriac' crosses my mind," the priest recalls. "A lot of the stuff she would say just wouldn't add up."

Sears, too, suggested Wantz might be helped by psychiatric care. She strenuously rejected the suggestion. "She was very opinionated about that," Sears says. "Everybody else was wrong and they didn't know."

The day before she died, during a videotaped session with Kevorkian, Wantz demanded that her body receive a "real complete autopsy" to find the source of her pain.

"I want it very detailed ... I want extreme, extreme," she told Kevorkian. "I want to be cut, like, 10 ways down here."

A thorough post-mortem examination, she was sure, would discover the real reason for her pain, possibly the barbed mystery object all her doctors had missed; in death, Wantz would be vindicated.

Wantz got the autopsy she wanted, but it yielded no evidence to explain her pain.

In a final blow, Wantz's lawyers abandoned the malpractice lawsuit she'd hoped would enrich her estate and punish Mercer. New evidence, they said, proved conclusively that neither Mercer nor his hospital had done anything improper.

Wantz's widower, Bill Wantz, never reinstituted the lawsuit. A year after Wantz's death, Bill Wantz married for a third time, wedding the next-door neighbor, Gast, whose sleep had been so disturbed by Marge Wantz's moaning.

Dr. Ljubisa Dragovic, still in his first year as Oakland County's chief medical examiner, got the call at his rambling Grosse Pointe Farms home just after 11 p.m. on Oct. 23, 1991.

When he drove into the Bald Mountain Recreation Area an hour later, at least five television news crews were there already, lighting up the surrounding woods like daytime.

The death scene was a bare, rustic, pine cabin favored by Cub Scout packs for weekend camping. No plumbing. No electricity.

On narrow cots were the bodies of Wantz and Miller, eerily illuminated by candles the deputies had lit. Wantz was still attached to the suicide machine with an IV in her arm; Miller wore a face mask attached to a canister of carbon monoxide.

After Adkins' death, Kevorkian had been eager to talk. Now, with Fieger calling the tune, neither Kevorkian nor the dead women's families responded to investigators' questions.

Warning that the Kevorkian "assembly line" was about to lurch into high gear, Thompson convened a grand jury and demanded that state lawmakers enact a clear prohibition of assisted suicide.

But if Thompson hoped to slow Kevorkian's pace, he was soon disappointed. Seventeen months had passed between Adkins' death and those of Wantz and Miller. The world had to wait only seven more months for the death of Susan Williams, a 52-year-old Clawson woman with advanced multiple sclerosis.

Then, five months later, the suicide doctor paid another house call.

Cancer wasn't the first setback life had dealt Lois Hawes.

A divorced mother of four, Hawes, 52, of Warren, had just started a new job when Guy, her second-youngest, sustained serious brain damage in a bicycle accident. Tethered to her home by his need for care, she cultivated a huge vegetable garden on the family's double lot. On Guy's behalf, she worked hard to secure programs for disabled kids in the local schools.

Hawes felt the first stabs of chest pain in late 1991. When a CT scan the following spring showed large tumors on her left lung and brain, she wasn't surprised to learn she was dying of cancer.

Cancer was the principal stalker and killer of Hawes' family. It had taken her father in the mid-'80s and her younger brother, Bob, just two years earlier.

Bob's death, especially, had shaken her. But instead of giving up her two-pack-a-day cigarette habit, Hawes talked to her older sister, Ann Pendzich, and they agreed they would not prolong the inevitable when their turns came.

Pendzich's came first. Hawes discouraged her sister from undergoing surgery, but Pendzich went ahead. She lost a breast and part of a lung — and survived.

But when Hawes' CT scans came back, her thoughts turned to suicide.

Any other decision would have been difficult. She had no medical insurance and no money. And Pendzich says, "When she found out it had spread to her brain, she thought that was it."

Hawes' daughter Stephanie called Kevorkian at her mother's request in mid-September. A few days later, Kevorkian convened the family for a videotaped counseling session around Hawes' kitchen table.

Kevorkian decided Hawes' death would be staged at the home of his long-time associate, medical supplies salesman Neal Nicol, who lived just north of Oakland County International Airport in Waterford Township.

Eager to bring his budding practice into the medical mainstream, Kevorkian talked to Hawes' doctors and arranged a last-minute session with a psychiatrist. Because Hawes found it difficult to walk, Dr. Seymour Baxter conducted his consultation in her car just before 6 p.m. on the night before her death.

The Birmingham psychiatrist found Hawes suffering from "a moderate degree of depression" but "mentally competent to make decisions," according to Kevorkian's notes, contained in police files.

The next morning, Hawes' 20-year-old-son, Robert, helped his mother up the front steps of Nicol's house. Lois Hawes looked tired and irritable as Robert and her sister settled her on Nicol's couch.

"Can I get you anything?" Kevorkian asked solicitously.

"Yeah," Lois Hawes rejoined with a smirk. "The gas."

She died of carbon monoxide poisoning at 10:45 a.m. on Sept. 26 on Nicol's sleep sofa.

Only two months later, Nicol's modest, wood-framed house was pressed into service again.

Catherine Andreyev, 45, from little Coraopolis in far western Pennsylvania, sat on the couch in Nicol's living room with a plastic mask on her face, breathing carbon monoxide and waiting to die.

Andreyev had been a preschool teacher, then a real estate saleswoman, until cancer took root in her breast and spread to her lungs, liver and chest. Bloated almost beyond recognition by chemotherapy, she was in nearly constant pain by the time she recruited two friends to drive her to her appointment with Kevorkian.

Now she drew long, painful breaths, sucking the gas deep into her ravaged lungs. But nothing happened.

"It's not working," she blurted finally.

"Keep trying," Kevorkian insisted. "Of course it will work."

Leslie DiPietro, a friend from Andreyev's college days, watched in increasing distress. "Poor Catherine was just struggling to breathe, because every breath was so painful.

"She was weeping; we all were," recalls DiPietro, a University of Michigan administrator.

After more time passed with no sign that Andreyev was being affected by the gas, Nicol, who usually procured the carbon monoxide for Kevorkian's suicides, checked the label on the canister and discovered the concentration of the gas was weaker than he'd requested.

Kevorkian, convinced he'd been sabotaged, was irate. "They did this on purpose!" he said angrily. According to DiPietro, Nicol shared Kevorkian's suspicion that the gas supplier had guessed the purchasers' intentions and deliberately substituted a dilute concentration.

After calming down, Kevorkian told Andreyev he had another canister containing the right concentration. "But you can stop this now," he added.

Andreyev, tears streaming down her face, told him she would continue. She died a few minutes later.

The very next day, Nov. 24, 1992, the Michigan House of Representatives passed a bill temporarily banning assisted suicide. The state Senate's approval followed nine days later.

But on Dec. 15, just seven hours before Gov. John Engler signed the temporary ban, Kevorkian presided over two more suicides.

Marguerite Tate, 70, had lived alone in Auburn Hills, estranged from her family and crippled by Lou Gehrig's disease. Marcella Lawrence, 67, who lived alone in Clinton Township, was afflicted with a variety of illnesses, from heart disease to liver cirrhosis.

Lawrence and Tate died together at Tate's home.

Since Adkins' death, it had taken the Legislature 2½ years to pass a bill to deal with Kevorkian's new medical practice. In the same time, Dr. Death had helped eight people die, all white women over 40.

The temporary ban on Kevorkian's new medical practice was destined to be the Legislature's last gasp, but Dr. Death was just getting started.

— *Kirk Cheyfitz*

A SUICIDE STREAK

JANUARY 1993-MAY 1995

Something inside Hugh Gale wouldn't let him sit still.

In the middle of the Depression, at age 13, after a stint in a foster home, he ran away from Detroit. Shucking the stepfather he couldn't stand, he headed west on the tops of boxcars.

After riding the rails all the way to California, he stayed with his grandmother for a while. Then he joined the merchant marine and sailed away.

Gale lived hard, traveled far, drank to excess in his youth, and smoked like a diesel truck until the moment he died. He married, fathered five boys, and divorced. When he remarried in 1971 at age 49, his new wife was half his age.

But the sailor with no formal education also loved painting pretty landscapes, playing his guitar and ukulele, and thinking about spirituality.

"His life sounds like a book," says Cheryl Gale, his widow. "He was a rebel."

The book of Hugh Gale's 70-year life had a hard last chapter. During his final two years, emphysema robbed him of breath, pushed his once-strong body into a reclining chair, and wouldn't let him up.

He was sitting in that chair in the living room of his Roseville ranch house when Dr. Jack Kevorkian paid a last visit early on Feb. 15, 1993.

Following what was, by now, a well-rehearsed routine, Kevorkian and two helpers set a white canister of carbon monoxide on the green living room carpet. Kevorkian shook Gale's large hand and said, "Are you sure?"

Then Gale fitted the plastic face mask over his mouth and nose and pulled a string to release the lethal gas flow.

What happened next, however, had nothing to do with Kevorkian's relentlessly promoted vision of physician-assisted suicide as a painless, peaceful death.

Within 45 seconds, according to Kevorkian's own notes, "the patient became flushed, agitated, breathing deeply, saying, 'Take it off!' "

Hugh Gale died about half an hour later, and Kevorkian set his sights on a double suicide scheduled to take place in three days.

But very soon after that, two different versions of Gale's interrupted, panic-marred death would be made public, creating a crisis for Kevorkian's rapidly running suicide machine.

As 1993 dawned, Kevorkian was facing a deadline.

Michigan lawmakers had moved to curb assisted suicide. Yet, for all its practical impact, they might have called their temporary ban the Suicide Acceleration Act.

The ban was scheduled to take effect March 30. But in the first two months of 1993, Kevorkian would assist seven more suicides — just one less than he had attended in the previous 30 months.

On Jan. 20 came Kevorkian's first male suicide — Jack Miller, 53, dying of cancer, isolated in his girlfriend's mobile home near Romulus.

Two weeks later came Stanley Ball, 82, and Mary Biernat, 74, both with cancer. Biernat drove from her Indiana home to Ball's house in Leland Township, where they died.

Deaths clustered more tightly. Elaine Goldbaum, a divorced 47-year-old immobilized by multiple sclerosis, died Feb. 8. She had been dispirited since her teenage daughter had been forced to give up caring for her. Alone, Goldbaum had been repeatedly victimized by hired caretakers. One stole her personal papers and another took her credit cards, burdening the dying woman with $20,000 to $30,000 in bogus charges, according to a relative.

Hugh Gale died a week later. Two Californians followed by three days — 44-year-old Jonathan Grenz and 40-year-old Martha Ruwart, both suffering from terminal cancer.

Everything seemed to be going smoothly until the evening of Feb. 25.

Around 7 p.m., more than a dozen police officers kicked open the locked front door of Neal Nicol's house in Waterford Township. Nicol, then 53, head of a small medical supplies company and a longtime Kevorkian friend, had assisted with the logistics of several suicides, including Gale's.

As Nicol's door flew open, another 10 investigators were combing Kevorkian's Royal Oak apartment.

Police were pursuing a lead from a right-to-life activist who, while sifting through Nicol's trash, had discovered Kevorkian's signed notes describing the Gale suicide.

The notes told how Gale had twice demanded the carbon monoxide mask be taken off and his suicide halted. The second time Gale cried "Take it off," he lost consciousness and the mask was left in place until his heart stopped beating some 11 minutes later, the notes said.

The document from Nicol's trash was even more interesting in light of an amended version discovered in Kevorkian's apartment. In Kevorkian's copy, the reference to Gale's second demand to halt was whited out. A new account — typed over the whited-out version — made no mention of a second protest.

To prosecutors in Oakland and Macomb counties, it looked like a possible cover-up. They announced a murder investigation. Kevorkian's lawyer Geoffrey Fieger countered with a late-night news conference where he dismissed the unaltered version of Gale's death as a typo and produced Gale's widow, Cheryl, to corroborate the amended account discovered in Kevorkian's apartment.

On Feb. 25, the same day police searched Kevorkian's apartment, Michigan lawmakers voted to make their suicide ban effective immediately.

Kevorkian vowed to defy it, but it would take him two years to complete his next seven suicides — the same number he had just run through in less than a month.

Gale himself would have been embarrassed by all the trouble his panic caused Kevorkian. Ironically, the suicide doctor had put off Gale's suicide several times, only to be pursued again and again for help.

Gale first noticed the shortness of breath in 1974. But even after doctors told him it was a progressive lung disease, he wouldn't give up his two-pack-a-day cigarette habit.

By 1985, Gale was on disability, unable to carry anything or climb stairs without gasping. Five years later, he was house-bound, tethered to an oxygen tank, and pining for the things he had loved — travel, painting and manicuring his perfect lawn.

Dr. Karl Emerick cared for Gale the last decade of his life and grew increasingly fond of the stubborn, rough-edged, but oddly sensitive patient who often resisted his instructions.

Emerick noted Gale's "increasing shortness of breath; really, really struggling, at times, to even walk a few feet."

Gale talked to his doctor for years about wanting to die, and Emerick, knowing his patient suffered bouts of depression, tried to get him to see a psychologist or psychiatrist. "He just wasn't willing to do that," the physician remembers.

One night in 1991, Cheryl Gale was awakened by her husband's voice, praying. Hiding in a corridor so as not to interrupt, she heard Hugh Gale say, "Please don't wake me up next time. Please, if there is a God."

Hugh began to think about people he had hurt in his life. He wished he could make amends. He wanted forgiveness.

"I was thinking about when my grandmother got so mad at me," he told Cheryl shortly before his death. They were at Stag Island, in the St. Clair River near Marysville, where his grandmother had a little shanty. Hugh was only 7, but the future mariner took the rowboat out on the water alone. "She got so mad, I was afraid to come back into the shore ... I thought she was going to spank me, and instead, she cried.

"She was so afraid for me," Hugh recalled. "My grandmother loved me and I shouldn't have done that."

Not wanting to cause any further pain to anyone, Hugh Gale probably would have been relieved when Macomb County officials concluded that he had wanted to die, and declined to prosecute Kevorkian.

Ronald Mansur rose before dawn on May 16, 1993. He didn't want to be late for his appointment with Dr. Kevorkian.

At 54, Mansur had weathered two divorces. Instead of the success he had wanted so badly, his business career brought him a 13-month prison term for fraud. Then came the cancer. When it spread to his bones, Kevorkian seemed the best of his dwindling options.

Mansur's sister, Jan Wilcox, accompanied her brother to his scheduled rendezvous at the family's real estate office on Detroit's east side, but Kevorkian was nowhere in sight. When about half an hour had passed, Wilcox called her mother, who called Kevorkian's sister, Margo Janus, who reached Kevorkian. Dr. Death had gotten the date of Mansur's assisted suicide mixed up.

"Jesus," Mansur said, "I can't even die right."

Mansur and his sister and the two friends there laughed, although Wilcox knew it was a nervous laugh.

Mansur said he was in pain and Wilcox gave him more morphine. They sat and waited in the back room of the real estate office.

Kevorkian had said Mansur's family and friends could face prosecution if they witnessed the suicide, so, after Kevorkian arrived, one by one they said good-bye.

Wilcox knew a hug would hurt Mansur — everything did. So she touched his hand and kissed him on the head and said, "You're so courageous. I love you."

Then she walked outside into the cold spring air without looking back.

"I couldn't turn around because I knew he would see me and I would see him and we'd both break down and his courage would go away."

When police arrived, they found Mansur sitting in an upholstered chair next to a cabinet with a bottle of morphine on it.

Later that morning, the publicity attending Mansur's death announced that Kevorkian was back in business, suicide ban or no suicide ban.

Three months later, Thomas Hyde, a 30-year-old with a long criminal record and Lou Gehrig's disease, became the youngest person yet to die with Kevorkian's assistance.

Heidi Fernandez, Hyde's girlfriend, faced the inevitable TV cameras with the couple's young daughter. Fernandez soon became one of the most visible advocates of Kevorkian's crusade.

As the months went by, Fernandez and others who were close to Kevorkian patients found solace in occasional potluck dinners at Neal Nicol's house, where four suicides had taken place.

Nicol had become indispensable to Kevorkian, attending pre-death counseling sessions with patients and families, inserting intravenous lines into patients' veins, helping to prepare the lethal drugs, and carrying bodies to cars.

Often it was Nicol who tried to ease the tension of final moments with his jovial death-bedside manner. It was Nicol who accompanied a grief-stricken Fernandez to Canada to scatter Tom Hyde's ashes. So naturally it was Nicol, a divorced father of two grown children, who hosted the survivor dinners.

Fernandez became something of a hostess at these gatherings, and soon she and Nicol became romantically involved, she says.

After three years, the relationship ended, but it had served an important purpose, Fernandez says. Staying close to "people associated with Jack Kevorkian ... was a way to keep myself close to Tom," she says.

As 1993 came to an end, the legal status of physician-assisted suicide was muddied by an ever-expanding cast of judges and prosecutors.

Kevorkian faced new criminal charges in Oakland and Wayne counties and went to jail briefly on two occasions, but the constitutionality of the Legislature's ban remained at issue. Kevorkian pronounced the legal wrangling irrelevant, but the flurry of assisted suicides slowed to a trickle, and in the next 16 months he would acknowledge attending only a single death.

Spring 1995.

In a one-bedroom apartment in Phoenix, Ariz., Nicholas Loving, 27, a big, athletic man who never managed to finish college or start a career, was dying by inches, afflicted with the incurable nerve disorder known as Lou Gehrig's disease.

Loving's family had hit the skids in 1971 when Nick was 4. His father, a U.S. Air Force man, divorced his mother, Carol, and disappeared from their lives.

The Lovings had never been affluent, but after the divorce Carol and her four children sank into poverty and welfare. Although the family recovered financially, the disaster created a close bond between Nick and his mother.

By his mid-20s, Loving still hadn't found himself. Living with his mother, he took some college courses and worked as a server at a popular sports bar and as a cashier at a gourmet grocery. Then, almost before his life had gotten started, it was over.

By the fall of 1993, Loving had been diagnosed with paralyzing, deadly amyotrophic lateral sclerosis. As his condition deteriorated, he told his mother he wanted to die. Carol Loving, who doted on her son, accepted his decision and soon made planning his death her primary focus.

About the same time Nick Loving told his mother he wanted to die, John Evans, then 77, a left-wing intellectual with two graduate degrees and a long history of fighting for social causes, was coming to a similar decision in Royal Oak.

Evans had earned his master's degree from the Harvard Divinity School almost four decades earlier. It might have seemed an odd degree for an atheist, but Evans saw the ministry as a way to put his liberal social ideas into practice in people's lives.

He became a minister in the Unitarian Universalist church, where many members do not believe in God. Then he resigned to devote himself to political activism. He opposed the Vietnam-era draft, helped to organize labor union locals, and lobbied to ban nuclear weapons.

"He was an atheist, but he was a religious man," says his widow, Jan Evans-Tiller, also a retired Unitarian minister, who now lives in Ithaca, N.Y. "He had a clear sense of firm beliefs leading to action."

In January 1995, Evans noticed he was getting very short of breath. He had no regular doctor, but found his way to a lung specialist, Dr. Robert Begle at William Beaumont Hospital in Royal Oak. Begle told Evans he was dying of pulmonary fibrosis.

There could not have been two more different people than Nick Loving and John Evans. But they shared a mistrust of doctors, a desire to control their final days, and the conviction that Jack Kevorkian could help them make a resounding statement with their deaths.

Kevorkian was trying, making phone calls and juggling schedules in an effort to orchestrate a double assisted suicide.

Jan Evans had objected reflexively to Kevorkian's request to assist side-by-side suicides in her home. "I couldn't imagine playing hostess on the same day I was becoming a widow," she told Kevorkian.

But her husband was more open to the idea, saying it might be an appropriate statement and an opportunity to "celebrate" the event with others.

As John Evans' appointed day in May grew nearer, he told Kevorkian he wanted to write letters to several Unitarian churches, challenging them to take a firm position on assisted suicide by providing "sanctuary" for his final minutes. But Geoffrey Fieger wouldn't allow it; if just one of the ministers Evans approached tipped off police or the press, the ensuing publicity could make Kevorkian's job more difficult.

Back in Arizona, Carol and Nick Loving were extremely enthusiastic about Kevorkian's plans for a double suicide. Like Evans, the Lovings believed simultaneous suicides would make a resounding political statement.

But when Carol Loving invited a reporter and a photographer from Phoenix's major daily newspaper, the Arizona Republic, to accompany her and her son to Michigan, Kevorkian was appalled. He decided against the double suicide and told the Lovings they'd have to reschedule Nick's death for another day.

It was an ironic role reversal. In the early days of his crusade, when many would-be suicides and their families recoiled from publicity, Kevorkian had preached the virtues of openness.

But as the legal assault on his activities continued, Kevorkian had dropped the role of flamboyant sidewalk preacher, loudly inviting the public's attention. Now, it was his two latest patients who pressed to turn their deaths into public testimony, while Kevorkian preached a brand new gospel — silence is golden.

Kevorkian and Nicol appeared at the Evans house in the predawn darkness of May 8, 1995. They hooked up the carbon monoxide and John Evans died, sitting in his favorite chair in the living room. Kevorkian was gone before the sun rose, as he had intended.

News of Evans' death angered and worried Nick Loving. "Is he going to do me or what?" he asked his mother testily.

But on the Wednesday two days after Evans' death, the Lovings got a call. Nick's death was on for Friday.

Having flown to Detroit, the Lovings met Kevorkian and Nicol in a motel parking lot on Friday morning and were driven to Nicol's house. There, comfortably arranged on a couch, Nick Loving put on his Walkman headphones, turned on "Dark Side of the Moon" by Pink Floyd, held his mother's hand, and began inhaling carbon monoxide.

His anger at Kevorkian was forgotten and he was a happy man, his mother says. Asked by Kevorkian if he had anything to "say to the world," Nick Loving repeated the lines of the old Negro spiritual, made famous by Dr. Martin Luther King Jr.:

"Free at last. Free at last. Thank God Almighty, I'm free at last."

— *Kirk Cheyfitz*

TWO WAYS TO GO

Dr. Jack Kevorkian uses two methods to help people commit suicide

CARBON MONOXIDE

1 A cylinder of the deadly gas is connected by a tube to a mask over the person's nose and mouth.

2 A valve must be released to start the gas flowing. Depending on the person's disablity, a makeshift handle may be attached to the valve to make it easier to turn. Or, with the valve in the open position, a clip or clothespin may be clamped on the tubing. Pulling it off allows the gas to flow.

By Kevorkian's estimates, this method may take 10 minutes or longer. Sometimes he encourages people to take sedatives or muscle relaxants to keep them calm as they breathe deeply of the gas.

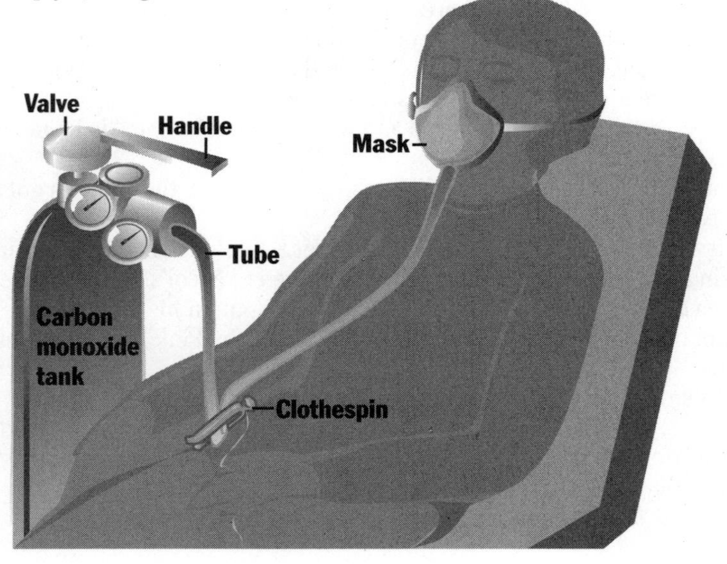

INJECTION

Kevorkian has built a device he calls the suicide machine. It has three canisters or bottles mounted on a metal frame, about six inches wide by 18 inches high. Each bottle has a syringe that connects to a single IV line in the person's arm. The first bottle contains ordinary saline, or salt water. Another contains sleep-inducing barbiturates, and the third a lethal mixture of potassium chloride, which immediately stops the heart, and a muscle relaxant to prevent spasms during the dying process.

1 Kevorkian or an assistant begins the saline solution flow.

2 The person who wants to die must deliver the barbiturates by throwing a switch or pulling a string.

3 After that, either a timer or a mechanical device triggered by the person's arm falling as the drugs take effect starts the lethal drug flowing. The idea is for the deadly chemicals to enter the bloodstream only after the person is asleep. Death usually occurs within two minutes.

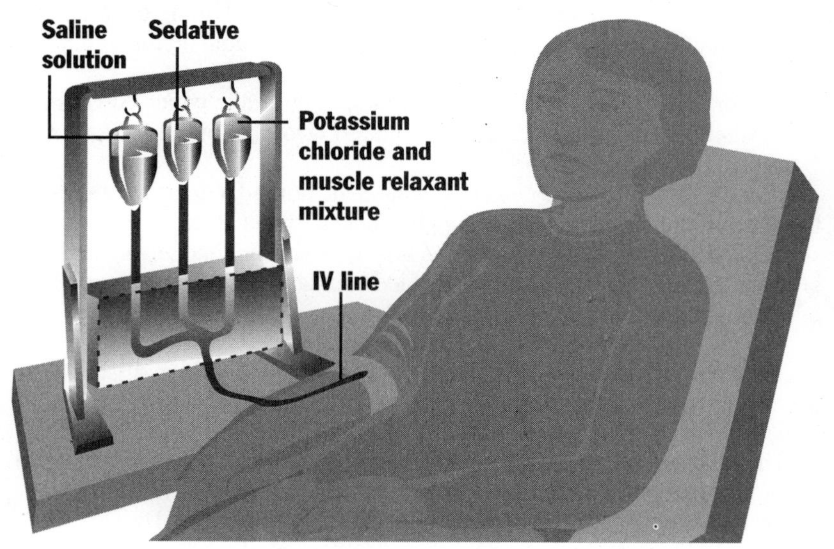

FOR SOME, IT WAS A PARTY

JUNE 1995-MAY 1996

Erika Garcellano could barely talk and had trouble scribbling notes on a legal pad. Ravaged by Lou Gehrig's disease, which attacks the spine and muscles, she slept in a recliner because she couldn't breathe lying flat.

"There is nothing graceful about dying with this disease," said her son, Paul.

And there was little gracious about the setting in which Garcellano committed suicide June 26, 1995, with the help of Dr. Jack Kevorkian.

Garcellano died in a flat-roofed, cinder block building Kevorkian had rented in northern Oakland County. Police found her thin body on a shower curtain thrown over a mattress on the bottom of an old bunk bed. A toilet bowl brush, mop and cleaning supplies were on a shelf next to the bed.

Kevorkian had partitioned the interior with old sheets and shower curtains. Mismatched carpet remnants covered part of the floor. The furniture was a yellow-and-white lawn chair, a wooden folding chair and an aluminum table, with a long-necked flashlight and a radio on top of it.

To some observers, the infamous Volkswagen van in which Kevorkian had assisted two previous suicides compared favorably to the stark scene of Garcellano's final minutes.

Yet, to Kevorkian, Garcellano's death represented a decisive step forward on the path to legitimizing physician-assisted suicide.

In his earliest writings about the subject, Kevorkian had envisioned a society in which the set of skills he called "obitiatry" would be sanctioned as a legitimate medical speciality.

Patients choosing to die would be referred to one of a small number of licensed clinics, where skilled practitioners would assist their suicides according to protocols as strict as those governing heart surgery or radiation therapy.

Thus, for Kevorkian, the significance of Garcellano's death scene: Where others saw a desperado's bivouac, stripped of whatever charm it had enjoyed during its previous incarnation as a hardware store, Dr. Death saw the first of the 21st Century clinics he had envisioned.

A bit rustic, perhaps. But four years after his first assisted suicide, he was leaving the world of battered vans and borrowed rooms behind. No longer would television cameras cluster outside his deceased patients' front doors, as they had in the aftermath of Kevorkian's numerous house calls.

In remote Springfield Township, Kevorkian hoped, physician-assisted suicide had found a permanent home. He called it the Margo Janus Mercy Clinic, naming it for his sister, who had died unexpectedly of a heart attack the previous fall.

The outside world may have regarded him as a maverick loner, but no one close to Kevorkian underestimated the importance of Janus' support.

To Kevorkian — who spoke of marriage in much the same way he spoke of a career in baseball broadcasting, as a remote possibility foreclosed in his youth — Janus was the only conspicuous source of female companionship as well as an invaluable ally.

She had been the silent partner in her brother's early crusade, helping screen those seeking his help, attending most of his assisted suicides, and comforting the survivors.

"Margo, although she was very supportive and sometimes may have even encouraged him where he didn't want to go, nonetheless had a civility about her, a kindness about her," said the Rev. Ken Phifer, a Unitarian Universalist minister in Ann Arbor who helped a member of his own church arrange a Kevorkian-assisted suicide. "Jack lost his better half when he lost Margo."

In June 1995, when Garcellano died, Kevorkian was still reeling from Janus' death, and still locked in combat with a prosecutor bent on imprisoning him.

More than anything, he said, he longed for other, reputable members of the medical community to rally to his cause.

But if Kevorkian harbored the hope that other doctors would volunteer to staff the clinic he had founded in his beloved sister's name, that hope proved short-lived.

After Garcellano's death, police closed the building and the owners ordered Kevorkian to vacate immediately.

During the next six months, still facing two criminal trials for assisting in suicides in Oakland County, Kevorkian would assist in only three suicides, and resort to leaving the bodies in places he expected them to be quickly found.

On Aug. 21, 1995, William Ferreras, a security guard at William Beaumont Hospital in Royal Oak, spotted a rusty silver 1986 Renault Alliance making several passes through the emergency entrance lane around 5:20 a.m. He could see that an older man was driving and an elderly woman was in the back seat.

The Alliance was followed by a small, four-door maroon car. Ferreras tried to flag them down, thinking the drivers needed help. But they passed him by and pulled into a section of the parking lot reserved for doctors.

The elderly man and woman got out of the Alliance and into the maroon car and drove away. Ferreras told another Beaumont officer to ticket the Alliance.

The officer did, leaving ticket #08058 on the car's fogged-up, dew-covered windshield.

About 90 minutes later, as the dawn burned off the dew, another security guard passed by the car and saw a body on the back seat, partially covered by a sheet. It was a woman, tall at 5 feet 9, bent head to knees to fit in the rear of the compact.

Michael Podeszwik, an investigator with Oakland County Medical Examiner's Office, noticed a white envelope stuck atop the dashboard on the passenger side. It was marked URGENT! in bright orange marker.

A note inside was signed by Esther Cohan: "Attend to me immediately in the silver car parked near the emergency room entrance."

Investigators traced the car's license plates to Kevorkian, who had purchased it six days earlier for $147 from Bob Saks Toyota in Farmington Hills.

On the radio that morning, Kevorkian attorney Geoffrey Fieger was identifying assisted-suicide No. 25 as Cohan, 46, of Skokie, Ill., a former Blue Cross & Blue Shield of Illinois secretary disabled by an advancing case of multiple sclerosis.

An autopsy confirmed that Cohan died of carbon monoxide poisoning. The Oakland County Medical Examiner's Office ruled the death a homicide, which was becoming its standard practice for Kevorkian deaths.

Cohan's body lay in the morgue for five days, marked Unknown Female #13. Her sister Judy had made the trip with her to Michigan, but did not identify or claim the corpse.

Finally, assured of Cohan's identity through numerous pieces of identification and photos faxed by the Ira Kaufman Funeral Home, the medical examiner released the body.

Judy Cohan spoke publicly about her sister for only a short time after the death. She said Esther wanted to die at home, but was afraid she would botch a suicide attempt.

"The only person out there who'd help her was Dr. Kevorkian," Judy Cohan said. "And she is at peace."

Esther Cohan had explained herself in a letter addressed "to all" that she wrote two weeks before her death.

"The ultimate act of love in ANY relationship is knowing when to say 'good-bye,' " she wrote.

"There's never a great time to go … but we all have to go sometime. The decision I made was for me! I don't expect others to live by my standards; nor can I live by others'.

"As things went from bad to worse and I was nothing more than a 'bed vege,' I knew it was time to say 'See ya!' To those who disagree — so be it — I know the people who care understand and that's all that matters!"

Following their investigation, authorities released the Alliance to Kevorkian. Less than three months later, he returned it, with another body.

At 9:25 a.m. Nov. 8, the Oakland County Morgue staff received a phone call directing them to a silver Renault parked outside.

The little car was still covered with black fingerprint powder from the police dusting after Cohan's death. It hadn't been washed since.

The body lying on the back seat, covered by a blanket, had a fresh 3-by-4-inch bump on the forehead. Dr. L.J. Dragovic, the Oakland County medical examiner, wondered if it had been dropped recently.

At 11:30 a.m., Nancy McDonald of Pacoima, Calif., came to the office to identify her sister, Patricia Cashman, 58, of San Marcos, Calif.

Like several of the women whose suicides Kevorkian had assisted, Cashman knew well the hardships chronic illness could impose on healthy family members.

A travel agent and writer who lived alone in a mobile home but traveled extensively until contracting breast cancer, she had spent part of her last healthy years looking after her cancer-stricken father.

In an emotional letter to Kevorkian the summer before she died, Cashman recalled the hundreds of sleepless nights she gave to her father's care and her bitterness after his death.

"I suddenly realized I felt some resentment about being there for him 24 hours a day and then seeming to have to sacrifice my own golden years," Cashman wrote.

Fieger said Cashman's cancer had spread to her bones, that she couldn't tolerate morphine and that she had lived in constant pain.

But the terror of becoming as dependent on others as her father had been on her was also a powerful factor in her wish to die.

"I also have been so concerned that I would wake up paralyzed and I will be at the mercy of others," she wrote in her letter to Kevorkian. "I have been pretty panic-stricken. Hopefully, with your assurance that you will help me, I can ease those concerns."

Two months later, the morgue phone rang again with news of a body in a car.

This time it was just before 6 a.m. on Jan. 29, 1996, and the vehicle was Kevorkian's white Volkswagen van.

Inside was the body of a woman, wearing a purple nightshirt and a robe, covered by a blue blanket.

Soon, Fieger was on the phone, saying the woman's family would come to the medical examiner's office to identify the body. Dawn Henslee identified the dead woman as Linda Henslee, 48, of Beloit, Wis.

Questioned later about leaving her mother in a rusty van on a cold morning in a strange place, Dawn Henslee reacted angrily.

"The TV reporters all focused on the van and made it sound so horrible that we left mom out in the cold like that," she said. "But, think about it: What's the first thing the medical examiner does? He puts the body in a refrigerator!"

Linda Henslee had lived with multiple sclerosis for more than 20 years. By the time she died, she couldn't walk, her speech was slurred, her vision had failed so much she couldn't read and she had big gaps in short-term memory.

An extremely independent person, Henslee had made it clear for two decades that she preferred suicide to the progressive debilitation she envisioned with MS. She vividly recalled attending an MS conference in 1980 where she was stunned to see the failing condition of people with advanced stages of the disease.

Instead, Henslee wanted to go out in style. The family celebrated her plans for several weeks and rented a white Cadillac to come to Michigan.

They spent four days together, going over family photos and assembling a scrapbook. Henslee telephoned family and friends all over the country. Her daughters recall her running up a telephone bill of several hundred dollars.

On her final day of life, her daughters decided to throw "like a birthday party" and went out and bought champagne, chilled shrimp, chocolate eclairs, strawberries and lottery tickets.

On Sunday the 28th, the Kevorkian crew returned to the motel room and helped Henslee's daughters move her to the location for the suicide. The Henslee daughters decline to say where their mother died.

But she was happy she finally got her wish.

She drank coffee, smoked a cigarette and died inhaling carbon monoxide with her daughters hugging her cheek to cheek — so closely that one

daughter got a pounding headache from the gas and had trouble standing.
"But it wasn't an ugly death," Dawn Henslee said. "We held onto her and talked to her until she was gone. And I'll never regret it. If I had to, I would help her die again."

Linda Henslee wasn't the only person to contact Kevorkian with big plans for dying. The next request for his help would make his assisted-suicide crusade an international affair.

Austin Bastable spent the spring of 1996 choreographing his death.

As he deteriorated from MS, Bastable helped write his eulogy. He taught his wife, Nina, how to handle their bank accounts and investments, something he had always done. He taught her how to program the VCR. He recorded a videotaped message to be played at a news conference after he died. He even instructed the funeral director to mold a smile onto his face.

Bastable's daughter, Jenni Macri, 26, said the smirk on her father's face sort of made his death easier to handle, because she knew he was getting what he wanted.

A Windsor, Ontario, toolmaker, Bastable, 53, had failed to kill himself with a drug overdose in 1994. For the last year and a half of his life, he was a crusader to change Canadian law that bans assisted suicide.

With the exception of his left arm, MS had paralyzed him from the neck down, leaving him unable to perform the most basic functions. He couldn't feed himself or wash himself or change his own underwear. He wore a catheter. A nurse manually extracted stool from his body.

"It's not an acceptable way of life to me," Bastable said so many times to the reporters he entertained in his living room as he pressed his assisted-suicide crusade in Canada. He never minded being the center of attention, not if it meant raising public awareness about assisted suicide. And then he would tell a joke or laugh at something he'd said and found especially witty.

In the end, he laughed at death, too.

A friend, Brian Keelan, picked up Austin and Nina Bastable at their house around 5 p.m. on May 6 and together they drove from Windsor to Michigan to meet Kevorkian. Keelan lied to guards at the border, telling them the group was going to Xochimilco in Detroit's Mexican Town for dinner.

Bastable laughed heartily — because it was a lie, and because his friend mispronounced the name of the restaurant.

When they arrived at the Farmington Hills home of Kevorkian ally Janet Good, Bastable sighed and said to his friend, "Well, bud, we've come a long way."

Good offered Bastable a drink. Her husband and daughter were there, as was Kevorkian, who had been testifying in his criminal trial for the deaths of Marjorie Wantz and Sherry Miller just hours before. Rounding out the gathering was a team of supportive doctors who examined Bastable and laughed at his jokes.

"I think you're saner than I am," one doctor said.

"I'm afraid to really ask this gentleman any questions," another doctor said. "I think he's more sane than any of us in the rest of the room."

Bastable grew tired of Kevorkian's repeated questions: Do you really want to die? Are you sure?

"You know, boys," Bastable said, "it's getting kind of late. I'm pretty pooped. Let's get on with it."

After a private talk with his wife, Bastable started the suicide machine.

A short time later — after Keelan told Kevorkian to make sure all the vials containing intravenous drugs were empty because "I didn't bring him here to go half way" — Bastable was dead.

One of Kevorkian's associates signed a death certificate and an Ontario funeral home took Bastable's body back to Canada. Word of his death leaked out the following evening.

Before he died, Bastable said he didn't want his "exit" to turn into a media event, although he must've known he was making his death one just as he'd made his life one.

Keelan, who spoke to dozens of reporters after Bastable's death, said what his friend really wanted was to spare his family from any unwanted attention.

And in the end, he got his way.

A group of reporters, whom Bastable had used to tell his story and who had used Bastable to tell a story, stood outside, in the rain, during his funeral.

They were not allowed in.

None of them heard Bastable's son-in-law proclaim that Bastable was finally "free at last."

— *Patricia Anstett*

KEVORKIAN KEEPS ON

AUGUST 1996-FEBRUARY 1997

L*auuuuuuura ... is the face in the misty light,* Pat DiGangi warbled from his motel-room bed. *Footsteps ... that you hear down the hall ...*

Sitting beside her husband, Ann DiGangi shook her head and smiled. It was the happiest she'd seen him in months.

Across the room, Dr. Jack Kevorkian was smiling, too.

"Sing it!" the suicide doctor urged. "Sing it!"

Like 20 pilgrims before him, DiGangi, a well-traveled history professor from Brooklyn, N.Y., had come to Michigan to die. Disabled and demoralized by progressive multiple sclerosis, he'd explored dying in Australia and the Netherlands, both of which made some provisions for physician-assisted suicide, before Kevorkian agreed to help him.

Now, as Kevorkian's video camera rolled, DiGangi was just hours from deliverance.

The conversation turned to big band music, a passion the two men shared. Kevorkian noted that DiGangi had once played the tenor saxophone.

"I also play alto," DiGangi said. Or at least he *had* played, he added modestly, in a big band. He'd even done some arranging.

But music making was another pleasure that had given way to his illness in recent years. DiGangi said he still liked to listen, but no longer had the energy to participate.

"Then what does that do?" Kevorkian asked, getting back to the business at hand. "Kind of ruins your life for you?"

DiGangi fell silent.

"Well," Kevorkian added quickly, "I don't want to put words in your mouth."

It was a little before dusk on Aug. 22, 1996, the busiest day of the suicide doctor's busiest summer.

That afternoon, he'd delivered the body of Patricia Smith, a 40-year-old Missouri mother whose multiple sclerosis had kept her confined to her home for more than two years, to Pontiac Osteopathic Hospital. Two days before that, he'd dropped off the corpse of Louise Siebens, a 76-year-old Texan who had suffered from Lou Gehrig's disease.

Now, in a room on the quiet side of the Bloomfield Township Quality Inn that had become his preferred site for assisted suicides, Kevorkian listened as Pat DiGangi detailed the case against his body.

Besides the MS, he had weathered two strokes, kidney cancer and surgery to repair an obstructed bowel. His legs were useless, his urine drained from a catheter, and he was nauseated by the myriad painkillers his doctors prescribed.

Though this was their first face-to-face meeting, Kevorkian had reviewed DiGangi's medical records and was clearly disposed to help him die. But first, he said, he wanted to go over some "hypothetical questions."

DiGangi, he noted, was too old to donate his organs. But, assuming he were younger, would DiGangi agree to be kept alive under general anesthesia until his organs could be harvested for transplant?

Alternatively, would he consent to being put under general anesthesia so doctors "could do an experiment on you that we can't do on humans now, either on your disease or any disease that you choose"?

"I'm not disposed to donate my organs," DiGangi answered warily. "Does that disqualify me?"

"No, no, we don't judge you on that," Kevorkian said. "These are just research questions."

The death of DiGangi and Smith — the 37th and 38th Kevorkian acknowledged attending — were among his least-noted.

Police and the news media were still preoccupied with No. 35, Judith Curren, amid news that the Massachusetts woman had filed domestic abuse complaints against her husband before taking her life. Her husband said the complaints were baseless, and were Curren's way of retaliating for his opposition to her desire to die.

Since Curren, Kevorkian and his attorneys had said very little about the people who came to him. Most of their bodies were delivered directly to hospitals with no explanation save an index card bearing their vital statistics and a one-line description of whatever had ailed them.

Police were left with no death scenes to investigate, no names of physicians who might confirm — or dispute — Kevorkian's claims. Friends and family members who had escorted a loved one to a furtive rendezvous with Kevorkian frequently left Michigan before police knew they had been here.

This marked a change for Kevorkian, who had preached openness about assisted suicide and bridled at one family's suggestion that they try to pass off an assisted suicide as a natural death.

"That's the last thing you want to do, is be secretive about it," Kevorkian told Lois Hawes' family in a 1992 consultation seven days before Hawes' assisted suicide. The law was clear — suicides had to be reported to police, and to mislead authorities about a cause of death would be to court prosecution. “All I have to do is do something illegal and they’ll have me in a minute,” Kevorkian said.

There was no practical way to conceal Kevorkian’s role in the deaths of people who came to Michigan for no apparent reason and died within hours of their arrival, frequently by carbon monoxide poisoning that left their skin a telltale red.

But Michiganders who sought Kevorkian’s help could be ushered to death in the privacy of their own homes. If sympathetic physicians could be found to certify their deaths as natural, there would be no pretext for nosy medical examiners to order an autopsy and draw their own conclusions.

Everybody in Ionia knew Loretta Peabody had suffered from MS for most of her adult life. Neighbors saw less and less of the 54-year-old housewife as the disease drew a noose around her modest world. By 1996, the only impression most people had was of a shriveled figure being helped into or out of a van that had been modified to accommodate her electric wheelchair.

To Peabody, it seemed clear her disease was souring her disposition as well as stealing her strength. In circumspect moments, she saw herself as a screechy harridan who made intolerable demands on her husband and children. Her illness, she said, was “a hardship on everyone.”

In a message videotaped four days before her death, Peabody counseled her husband, Joseph, not to feel guilty after she was gone.

“Think how bitchy I can be … You can’t get hell from me anymore,” she said.

Quietly, the Peabodys sought out Kevorkian, who arrived in Ionia on Aug. 30 with a video camera and his aide Janet Good.

“I can’t get a drink of water or go to the bathroom on my own,” Loretta Peabody told her visitors. “I have no dignity in my life.”

To her husband, she said: “If you find someone you care about, go for it.”

By the time Good and Kevorkian left, Peabody was dead.

Joseph Peabody assumed Kevorkian’s role in his wife’s death would remain private. There had been no corpse dropped off in the dead of night, after all. Loretta Peabody’s own doctor certified the death as natural, and her body was quickly cremated.

In quiet, conservative Ionia, where no one would ever figure on a suicide doctor making house calls, Loretta Peabody’s final hours seemed certain to remain a family secret.

They might have, too, but for a front-desk manager at a motel 100 miles away whose suspicions would lead police back to Joe Peabody’s door.

Wide awake and terrified in her Redwood City, Calif., hospital bed, Isabel Correa watched helplessly as Trino Soto turned to go.

No! she thought. *Don't leave me!*

The plea reverberated in her brain, but Correa couldn't speak. She wanted to run after her husband, but her legs were numb. She longed to reach for him, but she couldn't move her arms, or her hands, or her fingers.

Please! Don't go!

By the following day, Correa's body had shaken off its post-operative paralysis, but 2½ years later, when she asked Kevorkian to end her pain once and for all, the memory of those mute hours in her hospital bed still haunted her.

"I am rapidly reaching a point, I fear, of total paralysis," she told Kevorkian in a letter dated Aug. 2, 1996. "Please hear my plea, when I can still plead to you."

Correa, 60, had assembled seat belts and packed fruit in her native California before mysterious pain in her arms and shoulders cut her working life short.

The youngest of eight children born to Mexican immigrants, she never finished junior high school. She endured abuse in a marriage that ended in divorce, and was a widow from her second marriage when she met Soto, who would become her doting common-law husband.

Correa was savvy enough to sense that none of the myriad doctors she saw through Kaiser Permanente, the nation's model HMO, were seeing the big picture of her misery and fear.

So on July 12, 1996, a few months after the fourth in a series of largely ineffectual surgeries, Correa plunked down a $15 processing fee and demanded the voluminous medical records that documented her steady descent into a life of perpetual pain.

For two weeks she lay on her back in bed, scrutinizing the pages one by one. Some of the notes were beyond her ken, but slowly, some overarching patterns seemed to emerge:

Painkillers had been prescribed, deemed ineffective and discontinued, only to be prescribed again a few months later by a new doctor. Surgeries and therapeutic initiatives ended disappointingly. Hospital and emergency room admissions mounted, but seldom brought relief; in one instance the physician who signed Correa's discharge papers ruefully observed that her condition had probably deteriorated, rather than improved, during her stay.

Perhaps the most disturbing discovery was a notation, previously undisclosed, that Correa's neurologist planned to recommend another operation soon.

For Correa, who'd reaped only worsening pain from her surgeries, that was the last straw.

She told Soto and her closest sister that she had devised a bold, new course of treatment for herself. Then she shipped her medical records to Michigan and awaited a response from the only physician she trusted to render a second opinion.

To the children and grandchildren she'd kissed good-bye at a backyard barbecue the night before, Correa was a strong, stubbornly independent woman who'd seized control of her own destiny.

But to Neal Kassab, the 42-year-old front-desk manager at Kevorkian's favorite motel, the frail woman in a wheelchair was a damsel in distress — an innocent who might be dead before checkout time if Kassab failed to act.

He'd been suspicious of the trio from Fresno — the sickly Correa and the two sad-looking relatives who accompanied her — from the moment they'd walked in the door. They offered no explanation for their visit to Michigan, and the only thing they seemed interested in doing was getting back to the airport the next morning.

When they'd specified a first-floor room on the quiet side of Kassab's Quality Inn — the same location favored by other guests who'd died at the motel that summer, the manager handed them the key to Room 141, watched them leave the lobby and dialed the police.

I think we've got another one, Kassab told the dispatcher.

Before Kevorkian agreed to help her, Correa had often worried about how her last days would go. But she had never imagined she'd face the end this way: scalded by television lights in a motel parking lot 2,000 miles from home, her whole body throbbing as an angry man she'd never met trundled her wheelchair to and fro before the cameras, shouting about the Gestapo.

Correa just sat there, mute and mortified in her bathrobe, wondering what had happened to Kevorkian.

She didn't realize that two Bloomfield Township police officers had been watching her room since early afternoon. When Kevorkian and Good arrived, the cops moved in. Geoffrey Fieger, Kevorkian's lead lawyer, arrived a short time later with a TV news crew in tow, and soon the quiet death Correa had envisioned exploded into yet another bit of the improvisational theater that had punctuated Kevorkian's six-year crusade.

Other assisted-suicide hopefuls had gone before the cameras willingly, hoping to win Kevorkian's favor and law enforcement's forbearance. But Correa had never sought a public platform; she just wanted to die.

The following day, when all the cameras were gone and police seemed satisfied to have thwarted Dr. Death, he met her again and Correa got her wish.

At a news conference called to announce her death, Fieger hoisted the dead woman's pink sweater triumphantly before the cameras, calling it her "flag of freedom."

For Kevorkian, autumn unfurled in a familiar fog of deja vu: Defying all forecasts, Richard Thompson, the Oakland County prosecutor vanquished in summer's Republican primary, was gunning for the suicide doctor yet again, launching a final legal assault even as his subordinates jockeyed for position in the new prosecutor's administration.

From the moment he announced the newest charges against Kevorkian on Halloween, Thompson's indictment appeared doomed, a sort of prosecutorial Hail Mary pass destined to sail harmlessly over the head of his indifferent successor.

But in Ionia County, prosecutor Raymond Voet had opened a surprising second front.

A videotape confiscated in the police raid on Correa's Bloomfield Township hotel room turned out to include Kevorkian's exit interviews with four other people, including Loretta Peabody.

Police called on Peabody's startled husband and, by November, Voet was asking a grand jury to decide exactly how natural Peabody's death had been.

While new legal storms brewed, Kevorkian plodded on resolutely.

Jack Leatherman ... Richard Faw ... Wallace Spolar ... Nancy DeSoto ... Barbara Ann Collins ...

But the renewed furor was distracting, and Kevorkian slowed his frantic pace of summer.

On Nov. 7, after Ionia County detectives snatched him off the street without warning and rushed him to his second arraignment in eight days, Kevorkian seemed rattled. He conceded to the arraigning judge's condition that he not be present at any suicides while he awaited trial in Peabody's death.

The agreement took Kevorkian watchers by surprise. Why had he agreed to the moratorium, which he'd rejected in his Oakland County arraignment just a week before? Would he keep his word?

Publicly, at least, Kevorkian appeared to have taken a hiatus. November passed without a single assisted suicide, then December and January, although Good and Fieger said there were dozens of qualified candidates seeking Kevorkian's help.

Then, on Feb. 3, the bodies of two women from opposite coasts were delivered within hours to familiar venues: a New Jersey woman to Pontiac

Osteopathic Hospital and a California woman to the Oakland County Morgue, where she was left outside in the familiar Kevorkian van.

When investigators called to ask if his client was involved, Fieger just shrugged his shoulders. But he scornfully dismissed a suggestion that a Kevorkian wannabe was on the loose: "There's no copycat."

The whole country might be *talking* about physician-assisted suicide, after all, but Dr. Death was still the only one doing anything about it.

— *Brian Dickerson*

DEATH IS NOT FINAL

The aftermath stuns relatives who expected a conclusion

After Rebecca Badger killed herself, daughter Christy Nichols wanted to find the perfect memorial.

It had to be permanent. It had to be something that would reflect both the beauty of Badger's personality — when she was at her best — as well as the painful suffering they had shared before traveling to meet Dr. Jack Kevorkian in July 1996.

Nichols pondered for nearly a month, then chose an elaborate tattoo.

Nichols, of Goleta in southern California, had always enjoyed visiting the ocean with her mother. So she asked a tattoo artist in Santa Barbara to spread a scene of the ocean floor across the small of her back.

"There's a starfish and a sand dollar and there's a big seahorse with bubbles coming out of its mouth. It's really colorful and shows everything my mom would love," Nichols said.

To create this memorial, Nichols lay on a table through two hours of agony as tiny needles pressed the permanent dyes into her skin.

Thinking about the ocean, her mother and the pain, it became almost a penitential rite.

Ultimately, the pain grew so intense that Nichols had to stop the artist. Someday, she plans to go back and finish the memorial, adding the words: "In Loving Memory: Rebecca."

Nichols' experience of grief and guilt is typical of the aftermath for the dozens of people who have helped a friend or relative pay a fatal visit to Kevorkian.

The majority say they were satisfied with Kevorkian's services. He is quick, free, relatively painless and lethally effective. Most importantly, he has deflected authorities away from the families of his clients.

Kevorkian boasts that his methods are the most humane for all concerned.

However, the aftermath of the event often is far more disturbing than friends and relatives expect.

The pain and sorrow that follows any death in a family can become a traumatic ordeal when a media onslaught greets the grieving survivors, questioning their roles and pursuing details of the man called Dr. Death.

Often, the natural grieving process is delayed as survivors flee unwanted attention.

Neighbors and coworkers sometimes react callously to this controversial kind of death.

And, in many cases, the survivors discover that their lives are changed forever, in large and small ways:

■ Cheryl Gale — the wife of Hugh Gale, who ended his struggle with emphysema in February 1993 — says she fears that right-to-life activists might dig through the trash outside her Roseville home looking for evidence of her role in the assisted-suicide movement. So, Gale has taken to disposing of her personal mail by burning it in a coffee can in her backyard.

■ Jan Wilcox — the sister of cancer patient Ronald Mansur, who killed himself in May 1993 — now wears a reminder of her brother. Around her New York home, she pulls on the same thick socks that Mansur wore because his feet felt cold near the end of his life.

■ Carol Loving — the mother of ALS-sufferer Nicholas Loving, who killed himself in May 1995 — has devoted her life to lobbying for right-to-die legislation in Arizona, where she lives. Loving is a freelance writer and her campaign includes trying to produce a movie about her son's life.

The grieving process has been particularly difficult for these families. Many of them have tried to chart their course without the assistance of counselors or clergy.

As a group, the 47 people believed to have committed suicide with Kevorkian's help expressed ambivalence toward religion.

Only 14 of them, less than a third, said that organized religion played a significant part in their lives. At least 18 made it clear that they had little use for religion — and a few were openly hostile toward churches and clergy.

In at least 13 cases, the deaths were not followed by a funeral or memorial service, where loved ones could gather to mourn, often a helpful process in resolving grief.

"Bizarre" and "surreal" are words Dennis Garling uses to describe the aftermath of the death of his mother, Shirley Cline, a cancer patient from California who killed herself with Kevorkian's help last July.

Within hours of a Kevorkian-assisted suicide, survivors find themselves trying to grieve while surrounded by aggressive investigators, lawyers, reporters and advocates and opponents of Kevorkian's cause.

In many cases, this sense of isolation begins the moment Kevorkian tells the dead person's companions that they must help him dispose of the body.

After Cline killed herself in a motel, Kevorkian instructed Garling to push her body in a wheelchair into a hospital emergency room. Garling refused, so the task fell to Dorothy Wall, a friend who also attended the suicide.

Kevorkian insisted that Wall answer no questions at the hospital and wait for attorney Geoffrey Fieger to pick her up. Wall had to withstand two hours of intense pressure from doctors and security guards, who threatened to have her arrested. Finally, Fieger arrived and took her back to the Quality Inn.

Only a few hours had passed since Cline's death — but already Garling and Wall felt pursued like outlaws.

When they returned to Cline's house in Oceanside, Calif., the next day, they were shocked to discover a media encampment.

"When we hit the garage door opener and drove in, they just descended upon us and began asking questions to which we had no answers," Garling recalled. Reporters shouted at them and called them by name as they hurried into the house.

"That was a very alarming element for me," Garling said.

Three days later, a police officer telephoned Garling from Michigan and Garling did his best to answer the officer's questions.

But Garling said that conversation drew an angry rebuff from Fieger's law partner, Michael Schwartz, who was concerned about Kevorkian's legal status.

"Why did you open your goddamn mouth? You're endangering my client," Garling recalls Schwartz snapping at him.

Garling said that when he found himself attacked by people "who I thought were on my side, it made the whole thing very unpleasant."

Looking back, Garling described it as a "circus atmosphere" that left him emotionally scarred. "There is certainly an element of shame; there's an element of guilt; a whole host of negatives," he said.

Dr. Franklin Curren continues to talk to reporters, state investigators and anyone who cares to find out the details of his wife's complicated life.

He's been portrayed as a spouse abuser, a tax dodger and a twice-married man with big debts.

His wife's controversial death cost him his psychiatry job at a local hospital. They let him go with two months of severance pay, he said.

To practice medicine again — Curren holds physician licenses in Massachusetts and California — he also needs to straighten out misunderstandings with federal drug authorities who suspended his license to prescribe drugs on the basis of charges that he gave narcotics to his wife.

Her medical bills left the family in debt. Curren has daughters, 8 and 11, to support, and is trying to negotiate a settlement over back taxes with the Internal Revenue Service.

Curren said he warned his wife, Judith, that her death would create controversy. He feared some people would portray her as a depressed woman unable to make a rational decision about taking her life. He knew many people would never understand her complex disease, Chronic Fatigue Syndrome, that consumed both their lives for so many years.

Curren has detailed answers, charge by charge, for his wife's accusations that he beat her. The charges were fabrications from a woman, occasionally deranged by illness, in retalitation for his long opposition over her desire to take her life, he said.

He may not have been a perfect husband, but, he said, "I spent every living moment of my life taking care of Judy when I wasn't at work."

He bathed her, changed clothing she soiled because she could not move to a bedside commode, and assumed all the child care duties when he wasn't working.

Now, he must find another job.

Curren's daughter Catherine, who was 10 at the time of the suicide and wise for her years, analyzed the encampment of reporters outside the family home this way: "I get it," she told a friend. "We're the dart board and the press can throw darts wherever they want."

But her father looks at it differently. The media exposure wasn't the hard part, he said. "The hard part is what I went through with my wife."

The invasion of the media was especially agonizing for Christy Nichols — because reporters brought her shocking news about her mother.

Badger didn't have multiple sclerosis, the disease she cited in seeking Kevorkian's help. An autopsy found no sign of the MS, which leaves unmistakeable evidence on the brain.

Her doctors in California would later concede they were wrong in their diagnosis. In fact, for many years, Badger had been addicted to prescription drugs and suffered from psychological problems.

Nichols is haunted by the thought that her mother might be alive and well today if Kevorkian had insisted she consult another MS expert.

She sums up her Kevorkian-suicide experience and aftermath in one word: "Overwhelming."

Many Kevorkian clients painstakingly tried to script post-suicide events in an effort to soften the impact.

Elaine Goldbaum, an MS patient from Southfield who killed herself four years ago, encouraged her 17-year-old daughter to begin meeting with a counselor six months before the suicide.

Nevertheless, helping her mother kill herself and, afterward, suffering through the media frenzy was so unsettling for the girl that it took several years of therapy to help her regain her equilibrium.

"She's gone through some pretty heavy-duty counseling," Goldbaum's ex-husband said. "It's only been in this past year that she's returned to any kind of normalcy."

Few if any of Kevorkian's clients made more detailed plans than Linda Henslee of Beloit, Wis., who killed herself in January 1996.

Since 1980, Henslee had made it clear to her family that she would commit suicide before MS left her completely incapacitated. Her daughters, Dawn Henslee and Sherry Henslee-Johanson, had accepted their mother's plans years before anyone had heard of Kevorkian.

Linda Henslee asked for Kevorkian's help to shelter her daughters from possible prosecution.

When Kevorkian agreed, Henslee turned her attention to dozens of details. She wrote her own obituary. She planned her funeral. For two weeks before her suicide, she invited relatives and friends to gather around her bed in the house Dawn Henslee rents in Beloit to say their farewells.

Unlike most of Kevorkian's clients, Linda Henslee arrived in Michigan a few days early to spend more time with her daughters. Encamped in a motel room, the women made videotapes, sorted old photographs, organized a family scrapbook — and enjoyed their favorite foods: champagne, strawberries, shrimp and chocolate eclairs.

In spite of it all, Dawn Henslee said, the aftermath has been "the most horrifying experience that I've ever been through."

The invasion of reporters was disturbing — but just as troubling were the callous responses of other people.

Someone called Dawn Henslee's landlord and asked, "Is that house going to be for rent soon? You're going to kick them out now, aren't you?" In fact, the landlord was sympathetic to the Henslees, but the call was unsettling.

"For months, we didn't have time to grieve properly — and people didn't treat us like we were grieving, either," Henslee said. "The guy who came to pick up the hospital bed that mother had used, told us: 'Normally, I would say I'm sorry, but I guess this is what she wanted.' He didn't think this was a loss for us.

"When the nursing agency sent someone over to pick up mother's motorized cart, all they said was, 'Thank you for not implicating us.' "

A year later, Dawn Henslee and her sister still have not come to terms with their grief — or their anger over this kind of cold treatment. Mainly, they wish they could have avoided the Kevorkian spotlight.

"If we could do it over again, we would do it here at home, regardless of the legal consequences," she said.

Other friends and relatives of Kevorkian clients, including Carol Loving in Phoenix, have channeled their energies into right-to-die activism.

Nicholas Loving was only 27 when ALS left him bedridden and unable to speak clearly or to use his fingers. Also known as Lou Gehrig's disease, ALS is a degenerative spinal cord and muscle affliction.

Loving became so frustrated that he made three unsuccessful attempts to kill himself in his mother's apartment, where he lived. Carol Loving said she regards Kevorkian as Nicholas' savior.

"I'm Nick's mother, but I'm also a writer," she said. "Now, it's my mission to tell Nick's story and see laws changed on this. I know that Nick's story will become both a book and a movie. ... If people can just see how someone so young suffered so intolerably, they'll know that we have to change these laws."

But even that activism doesn't soften the grief over his death.

"I'm so grateful that Dr. Kevorkian helped Nick and there is just no changing that, because that took the responsibility off me," Loving said. "But I'm still mourning Nick. I just can't get over it."

Carol Loving has become obsessed with her son's ashes.

On May 12, the one-year anniversary of the suicide, several relatives planned to carry out Nick's wishes by sprinkling his ashes from a mountain top. But Carol was not ready to give up all of the ashes and, instead, took a small spoon and measured out 23 scoops of the ashes for the mountain-top rite.

Why 23? "Because Nick was No. 23 in Dr. Kevorkian's series," Carol Loving explained.

As she examined the ashes, she discovered small bone fragments, some of them white and some of them charred black.

"Now, I carry around two bone chips with me, one black and one white," she said. "I just keep them in my pocket. This way, any time I put my hand in my pocket, there's my son. It's pathetic, but when it's your son, you just don't get over it."

Other relatives and friends of Kevorkian clients are moving in the opposite direction — trying to resolve their grief by distancing themselves from the assisted-suicide cause.

One of the most outspoken Kevorkian supporters in recent years has been Heidi Fernandez, the fiancee of Thomas Hyde of Novi, an ALS patient who killed himself in August 1993.

After Hyde's death, Fernandez showed up wherever necessary to publicly defend Kevorkian. For more than three years, Fernandez said the same things many survivors say: Kevorkian offers sick people control; he is a savior.

Now, however, Fernandez says she has grown weary of all the arguments over assisted suicide. "Nobody's ever going to agree on this subject."

She has decided she will make no more public statements in defense of Kevorkian.

"I thought that if I kept in the forefront, it was going to keep me close to Tom, when in fact I was distancing myself from his memory. I was in an arena that was unfamiliar to both Tom and I," Fernandez said.

"We didn't go to courtrooms and sit in front of TV cameras and things like that. Tom would not even probably know me any more.

"I need to get back to my life."

— David Crumm

GABRIEL B. TAIT

Dr. Jack Kevorkian cracks a joke for journalists outside 48th District Court in Oakland County on Oct. 31, 1996, as he was arraigned on charges stemming from 10 assisted suicides.

PART TWO

THE ISSUES

HE BREAKS HIS OWN RULES

Through almost seven years of helping people kill themselves, Dr. Jack Kevorkian has consistently violated most of the rules and standards he publicly claims to follow.

Engaged in a crusade to legalize physician-assisted suicide, the onetime pathologist and his lawyer, Geoffrey Fieger, have insisted Kevorkian follows strict guidelines.

But those claims do not hold up. Actually, Kevorkian appears most consistent at ignoring the rules he has written or endorsed, a Free Press investigation shows.

Kevorkian declined invitations to discuss the Free Press findings. But Fieger conceded in a recent interview that Kevorkian has found it hard to follow his "exacting guidelines" in an atmosphere of "persecution and prosecution."

"He's proposed these guidelines saying this is what ought to be done," Fieger said. "These are not to be done in times of war, and we're at war."

In reviewing the lives and deaths of 47 people whose suicides have been publicly linked to Kevorkian since June 1990, Free Press reporters interviewed hundreds of people and examined thousands of pages of documents, including medical records, autopsy reports, marriage and divorce records, police files, personal notes and letters.

The investigation also debunks perceptions that Kevorkian only helps people who are terminally ill — likely to die within six months — or are in agonizing pain.

In fact, at least 60 percent of Kevorkian's suicide patients were not terminal. At least 17 could have lived indefinitely and, in 13 cases, the people had no complaints of pain.

Many friends and relatives of the people who committed suicide with Kevorkian weren't even aware he had a written set of standards. But they believe he is willing to suspend almost any rule to accommodate people who really want to die.

"What comes across in the public as almost a fanaticism comes across in private as a wonderful eagerness to perform a service that he's convinced should be available to people," said Jan Evans-Tiller, widow of retired Unitarian minister John Evans, who died with Kevorkian's help.

Examining the Kevorkian suicides, the Free Press found that in clear violation of his own written standards:

KEVORKIAN HAS FAILED to consult psychiatrists, even when dealing with depressed people.

In a 1992 article setting out his rules for physician-assisted suicides,

Kevorkian wrote it is always mandatory to bring in a psychiatrist because a person's "mental state is ... of paramount importance." But the Free Press found at least 19 cases in which Kevorkian did not contact psychiatrists.

In at least five of those cases, the people who died had histories of depression.

KEVORKIAN HAS FAILED to observe minimum waiting periods before helping people to die.

He has stated that after signing a formal request, a person must always wait at least 24 hours before getting help to commit suicide. But the Free Press found at least 17 instances in which Kevorkian's first meeting with the person was also his last. In at least five of these, less than three hours passed from the signing of the request to the moment of death. In one case, the waiting period was one hour.

KEVORKIAN HAS FAILED to consult with pain specialists and other medical experts, even when the need was clearly indicated.

Kevorkian has endorsed a written rule requiring that a pain expert be consulted in any case where "pain is a major factor" in a suicidal patient's complaints. But out of 33 cases in which people came to Kevorkian complaining of chronic pain, he failed to consult a pain specialist in at least 17.

KEVORKIAN HAS FAILED to discover financial or family problems that may have contributed to a patient's wish to die.

He has written that skilled help is "necessary to detect personal or family disputes, to clarify financial problems" and help people with their wills and funeral arrangements. But his questioning in these areas is cursory at best. In one recent case, he failed to uncover multiple allegations of spousal abuse and debts of more than $320,000.

Kevorkian outlined these and other rules in a 1992 article he wrote for the American Journal of Forensic Psychiatry. Fieger has described the article as a codification of the guidelines Kevorkian lives by.

In an essay last August in USA Today, Fieger wrote that Kevorkian also "scrupulously follows" the 10 guidelines of Physicians for Mercy, a group of doctors who support physician-assisted suicide.

But in his recent interview with the Free Press, Fieger said it is often "not practical" for Kevorkian to follow the safeguards he has publicly embraced.

Psychiatrists and pain specialists are frequently reluctant to cooperate, Fieger said. In some cases, he added, a person's competency is so "obvious" that a psychiatric exam is unnecessary.

Fieger acknowledged the importance of the 24-hour cooling-off period Physicians for Mercy has prescribed for people seeking physician-assisted suicides. But he said the threat of police intervention has made Kevorkian reluctant to delay.

"Some patients don't want to wait," Fieger said.

Though Kevorkian and Fieger say the suicide doctor "counsels" all his clients extensively, the Free Press found numerous cases where contact was extremely brief, and focused mainly on scheduling and logistics for the suicide meeting.

Kevorkian has written that if a person seeks help committing suicide and then "manifests any degree of ambivalence, hesitancy, or outright doubt with regard to her original decision, the process is stopped" and the person can never again be considered for assisted suicide.

Yet Kevorkian didn't respond when one of his early candidates made an ambivalent statement about her desire to die.

It was Oct. 21, 1991, and Kevorkian was on the phone with Marjorie Wantz, 58, who lived in Berrien County. She complained of constant vaginal pain and was scheduled to die in two days.

The main purpose of the phone call was for Kevorkian to discuss directions, schedules and inexpensive motels with her husband, William, who would drive her to the Detroit area. But at one point, Bill Wantz put his wife on the line.

"Have you thought this over well?" Kevorkian asked.

"Yes, I thought it over well," she replied, according to a transcript of the conversation prepared for an Oakland County grand jury. "I got two choices. Either stay like this or go with the other way."

Kevorkian never asked Wantz what she meant. Instead, he replied, "You sound like you're in pain."

Marjorie Wantz replied, "I am in pain. I'm in pain and I'm getting nervous."

Kevorkian then asked one question about her doctors and pressed ahead with the logistics of her death.

Dr. Kalman Kaplan, a psychologist and expert in suicide prevention counseling, has read the transcript.

"It's not a genuine consultation," Kaplan said.

"When somebody says 'I could go two ways,' my first reaction is, 'It sounds like you're confused or ambivalent' ... He doesn't explore those points ... He doesn't draw her out."

Kaplan, who is studying Kevorkian's methods, has reviewed 14 videotapes made by Kevorkian of conversations with 12 people wishing to die.

"There are aspects of counseling in some of them," Kaplan said. "But in many of these tapes, it's difficult to see."

Kevorkian did ask Hugh Gale, a 70-year-old Roseville man suffering with emphysema, to make a list of things he enjoyed so he would have reasons for living. And there are numerous cases where Kevorkian has told people they are not ready to die and has put them off for days, weeks or even months.

But in many cases Kevorkian's conversations with his patients focused on negatives — the things they couldn't do, rather than potential reasons to live.

Kaplan, head of the Suicide Research Center at Chicago's Columbia-Michael Reese Hospital and a psychology teacher at Wayne State University, cited a taped session with Janet Adkins, the 54-year-old Portland, Ore., woman who was Kevorkian's first suicide. Three days earlier, the Alzheimer's disease patient had beaten her son at tennis.

Rather than her tennis ability, the conversation focused on memory lapses that made it hard for Adkins to keep score on the court.

The Free Press found that Kevorkian's patients and practices vary wildly.

— From terminal illness to no physical illness: He has assisted in the deaths of elderly, terminally ill and desperately suffering men and women, such as Merian Frederick, who died Oct. 22, 1993, at age 72, unable to speak, eat or swallow because of the fatal, paralyzing nerve disease ALS, also called Lou Gehrig's disease.

But Kevorkian also helped end the life of at least one woman, 39-year-old Rebecca Badger, who was a mentally troubled drug abuser and had no physical disease. An autopsy showed she was mistakenly diagnosed with multiple sclerosis.

— From years of counseling to minutes: Kevorkian has had at least three cases in which more than a year went by between his first contact with the suicide candidate and the moment of death.

He saw Margaret Garrish in her home in Royal Oak at least three times in two years before she died there in November 1994, legless, partially blind and crippled by arthritis.

But Kevorkian accepted Adkins as his first patient without ever speaking to her, only with her husband. Even when Kevorkian finally met Adkins, just two days before her death, he "made no real effort to discover whether Ms. Adkins wished to end her life," the Michigan Court of Appeals stated in a 1995 ruling upholding an order against Kevorkian's activity.

— From hundreds of pages of medical records to one or two as a basis for life and death decisions: Isabel Correa, a 60-year-old woman from

Fresno, Calif., sent him a 216-page medical file before Kevorkian agreed to help her die.

Shirley Cline, 63, an Oceanside, Calif., woman with terminal bowel cancer, sent only a one-page summary of her medical history.

Even when Kevorkian has voluminous medical records, it's not clear how he uses the information. For example, though Correa's main complaint was severe pain, her records make no mention of any consultation with a pain expert and Kevorkian never referred her to a pain specialist.

Very often, when Kevorkian has tried to consult with a patient's doctors, he has been turned down. But from the very beginning, he has shown a tendency to simply dismiss opinions different from his own.

One of the few cases in which Kevorkian did consult was Adkins'. He spoke with Dr. Murray Raskind, a psychiatrist who had been treating her at the University of Washington Hospital in Seattle, and a nationally recognized expert on aging and Alzheimer's.

Raskind told Kevorkian that Adkins was not competent to make a life-and-death decision. Kevorkian gave her a lethal injection anyway, writing later that his opinion was based solely on conversations with Adkins' husband.

Kevorkian broke his rules even in an early case when he was making a point of trying to stick to them.

When Susan Williams wrote Kevorkian in late 1991, saying, "I'm asking you to help me commit suicide," he was on the brink of an important event — the publication in a medical journal of his plan to create a new field of "obitiatry."

Kevorkian's lengthy article, "A Fail Safe Model for Justifiable Medically-Assisted Suicide," has consistently been cited by Fieger and Kevorkian as the definitive statement of Kevorkian's standards.

Kevorkian decided Williams would be his model case.

"In a way, you're making history here," he told her family during the first of three lengthy videotaped sessions he conducted in spring 1992.

But Kevorkian's new rules were quickly cast aside.

It is not known whether Williams, 52, of Clawson, crippled by multiple sclerosis and blind, was clinically depressed. Her grown son and only child, Dan, believes she was. Her physician at William Beaumont Hospital in Royal Oak had recommended she see a psychiatrist.

Williams even told Kevorkian, "What depresses me is when the sun shines" because she couldn't go outside.

At one point, Kevorkian said, "I'd like to have a social worker interview you." His article had said such consultations must be conducted.

He also said he'd like to have "another psychiatrist and neurologist here to make sure there's no morbid depression," again following the rules.

But at the next videotaped session, on May 3, Kevorkian announced he was dispensing with any psychiatric consultation because Beaumont Hospital had told him psychiatrists don't make house calls.

"I know she's sane," he declared. "Everybody does. This is just for the record."

There were no other consultations. At the third and final videotaped conference, the main topic was when Williams should die.

Several years later, in 1995, Kevorkian would endorse a rule requiring that "the time and site" of suicide are solely up to the patient.

That was not true for Williams.

Her sister Nancy Vervaras preferred Friday, May 15.

"I was thinking Wednesday," said Williams.

Kevorkian interrupted her: "I was thinking Sunday ..."

In the end, Susan Williams, who wanted to die at night, on a Wednesday, died at 10:43 a.m. on a Friday, May 15, 1992.

Carol Poenisch has a personal and political interest in assisted suicide.

She is the youngest daughter of Frederick, the 72-year-old Ann Arbor homemaker and social activist who died of carbon monoxide poisoning in an unoccupied apartment in Kevorkian's threadbare Royal Oak apartment building.

Poenisch is a leader of Merian's Friends, a group working to put a proposal legalizing assisted suicide on a Michigan ballot.

As one of her mother's primary caretakers, Poenisch became an insider in Kevorkian's world before her mother's death, and a close supporter afterward. She is on the executive board of the Michigan Hemlock Society, a branch of the national right-to-die organization.

Poenisch, 42, with a graduate education in public health, has a unique perspective on Kevorkian.

She wants physician-assisted suicide legalized — and regulated. But Poenisch said she believes the only regulation Kevorkian will ever adhere to is his own personal judgment.

Under Kevorkian's real rules, "you can't make a generalization about who would get this and who wouldn't," she said. Only Jack Kevorkian gets to decide.

"He believes that it's case by case," Poenisch said. "I think that's what he really believes."

— *Kirk Cheyfitz*

STANDARDS SET ASIDE

"I have never met any doctor who lived by such exacting guidelines as Kevorkian," Jack Kevorkian's attorney, Geoffrey Fieger, wrote in a 1996 essay for USA Today. "He published them in an article for the American Journal of Forensic Psychiatry in 1992. Last year he got a committee of doctors, the Physicians for Mercy, to lay down new guidelines, which he scrupulously follows."

But a Free Press investigation of Kevorkian-assisted deaths found that Kevorkian frequently ignores his own rules — and Fieger now contends Kevorkian can't be expected to observe them consistently until physician-assisted suicide is legalized.

WHAT KEVORKIAN SAYS

Every assisted-suicide candidate undergo extensive counseling with Kevorkian.

Every candidate for assisted suicide must be examined by a psychiatrist.

Patients who complain of chronic pain should be examined by a doctor who specializes in pain control.

Before agreeing to assist a suicide Kevorkian makes a detailed review of each patient's medical records.

Those who qualify for Kevorkian's help suffer from afflictions that are incurable or cannot be treated without intolerable side effects.

Death should not take place sooner than 24 hours after a patient has made a final request.

WHAT THE FREE PRESS FOUND

Counseling is often limited to phone calls and brief meetings that include family members and friends.

There was no psychiatric exam in at least 19 Kevorkian assisted suicides, including several in which friends or family reported that the patient was despondent over matters other than health.

In at least 17 assisted suicides in which people complained of chronic pain, Kevorkian did not refer the patient to a pain specialist.

Kevorkian's access to such records varied widely; in some instances, he received only a brief summary of the attending physician's prognosis.

Autopsies of at least three Kevorkian suicides revealed no anatomical evidence of disease.

At least 19 patients died less than 24 hours after meeting Kevorkian for the first time.

DOCTORS' PROPOSAL

An organization called Physicians for Mercy, stressing that it was not a support team for Dr. Jack Kevorkian but a group of doctors who had examined the issues, proposed in 1996 these guidelines for physician-assisted suicide:

- A request for medical help in dying must be made voluntarily by the patient. No one can make such a request on the patient's behalf.
- The request must be made in writing, signed by the patient and any doctor involved, and witnessed by two adults with no financial interest in the patient. All signatures must be notarized.
- The request must be forwarded to an obitiatrist, a physician who specializes in helping people kill themselves.
- That doctor must refer the request to at least two consultants.
- The patient must be seen by at least two doctors. One must be a specialist in the disease afflicting the patient. One must be a psychiatrist. If pain is involved, the patient also must be seen by a pain specialist.
- The patient must be confirmed to be competent, incurable and in uncontrollable agony.
- The consultants must agree and report in writing that the patient is mentally able to make an informed decision, is suffering from an illness that cannot be cured, and is in agony that cannot be relieved or controlled through methods acceptable to the patient.
- The patient must review the consultants' reports either with the obitiatrist or with a doctor of the patient's choosing.
- The patient must choose the time and place of death within three weeks of reviewing the consultants' reports. This final request and statement of choices must be made in writing and witnessed the same as the original request.
- Death cannot take place sooner than one day or later than three days after the signing of the final request.
- The patient can halt the process at any time.
- The obitiatrist will not charge any fee for the final act of helping to administer a lethal agent.

THE FAILURE OF MEDICINE

Susan Williams had severe skin problems and asthma and was legally blind. She needed a catheter to keep herself dry. She was in a wheelchair and endured painful muscle spasms from a worsening case of multiple sclerosis.

For eight years, she saw the same doctor, who, in the view of Williams' family, provided only cursory care.

Most of her visits lasted no more than five to 10 minutes, consisted mostly of general questions to Williams, and never involved a thorough physical exam, according to Williams' sister and her son Dan, who said he always accompanied his mother into the examining room.

When Williams said she was depressed, just existing day to day, the doctor suggested she see a psychiatrist.

When Williams said later that, instead, she had called Dr. Jack Kevorkian about suicide, her son remembers that the physician told him: "If I was in your mother's shoes, I'd probably do it too."

Williams, a Clawson homemaker, was 52 when she died with Kevorkian's help in 1992.

Her experience with the health care profession, as recounted by her family, is similar to that of other people who asked Kevorkian to help them die. Interviews with friends and relatives, medical records, videotapes the people made with Kevorkian and other material reviewed by the Free Press point to failures of medicine that left people feeling stressed, hopeless and abandoned.

The problems they describe paint a picture of doctors, home-care agencies and social services programs falling badly short of the needs of people with chronic and terminal illness.

Some patients or their families even described Kevorkian as the first doctor they had encountered who seemed to care, and who listened to them.

Kevorkian was certainly the only doctor any of the families had known who made a point of refusing money for services rendered.

In fact, several people who turned to Kevorkian chose death, in part, because, lacking money and health insurance, they could not afford medical interventions that would prolong their lives.

There is no disputing that some of the people who turned to Kevorkian had very difficult medical situations. Nine, for example, had ALS, or Lou Gehrig's disease, which progressively attacks the spine and muscles but is often confused with a stroke or arthritis; another had Chronic Fatigue Syndrome, which can appear to be depression.

But for others, according to doctors, life could have been bearable with better pain relief, better coordination between specialists and primary doctors, and a more caring attitude from physicians.

Would that have been enough to stop a suicide decision by someone with, say, a progressing disability? Perhaps not.

But Dr. Howard Brody, a medical ethicist, believes that good care from skilled, compassionate doctors would make a difference for 97 out of 100 people.

"If you don't listen carefully to what a person's needs are, and try to figure how to meet those needs, you can have people suffering even though, technically, they are getting good care," said Brody, a Michigan State University physician who chairs the medical ethics committee of the Michigan State Medical Society, the state's largest physician group.

Brody said he's "a little horrified" by doctors who do nothing when they find out that their patients are contemplating Kevorkian.

In fact, patients who are dying or suffer from incurable chronic illness need a doctor's attention and concern more than ever, he said.

"That's why Kevorkian is seen as such a savior, but medicine truly has abandoned them," Brody said, calling the popularity of assisted suicide "one of the most serious indictments we have today of medical practice."

The failure of medicine is just emerging as an issue in the national debate over assisted suicide.

The following cases, and the underlying issues they address, could figure into the debate.

With Susan Williams, "It got to be a waste of time to take her to the doctor," said her sister Joanne Gibbons of Redford.

Williams' son Dan said she was diagnosed with MS 12 years before she died. He said her doctor at the time told her not to go to MS clinics because she would see severely disabled people and find it depressing.

Williams had numerous red, blistery wounds from eczema, a skin disorder. She was prone to bedsores and at risk of infection from the catheter. Her husband, 30 years older and suffering from a heart disorder, struggled to help with her care.

One day her sisters called 100 agencies to see whether volunteers were available to come into the home, even for a few hours, but they found nothing, Gibbons said.

Williams was a member of the Michigan chapter of the National Multiple Sclerosis Society, but when she turned to it for help, her family said, she was told her household income was too high to qualify for even a wheelchair. The Williams family lived on Social Security benefits, an income

depleted by huge bills for prescriptions not covered by Medicare.
The family could only afford a nurse's aide for a few hours a week.
"There's not a lot of help unless you can pay for it," Gibbons said. "It turns you sour on the whole medical profession."
The MS society said Williams was approved to receive some services, but it declined to be more specific.
Spokeswoman Alana Noble said she understood the family's anger. "We're not going to argue with the family of someone who died of MS," she said.
Dr. Lawrence Eilender, a Birmingham physician who was Williams' primary doctor for the last eight years of her life, declined to discuss his treatment of her.

Isabel Correa, 60, of Fresno, Calif., was increasingly paralyzed and in pain when she agreed to surgery to remove a noncancerous tumor that had been growing at the base of her skull for at least five years. Without the surgery, she eventually would have become a quadriplegic, her doctors said.
Afterward, she was "markedly weaker" on one side of her body, with burning sensations and pain, medical records show. The records list her condition on discharge as worse than when she was admitted.
Correa eventually recovered from that operation, but a year later, her upper spine was so distorted that she suffered severe weakness and relentless pain. To straighten her spine, doctors did more surgery, fusing a chip of her hip bone into her neck and inserting a metal strut.
For stability after the surgery, they put her in a halo, a metal frame that was screwed into her head and rested on her shoulders; she had to keep it on day and night.
Given only ordinary Tylenol for pain, Correa recuperated for a while in a nursing home that she found depressing and terrifying, said her husband, Trino Soto.
Finally, her pain grew so severe that she begged doctors to remove the metal contraption she had worn for almost three months.
When she was finally back home with Soto, she told him: "Honey, first thing we're going to do, we're going to put in for my medical records."
When Correa reviewed them a few days later, she discovered that doctors were planning another operation they hadn't told her about.
Convinced the surgery would do nothing to assuage her pain, Correa sent her records to Kevorkian and asked for his help.
Correa's medical care was provided through the Kaiser Permanente health maintenance organization in California. She saw various doctors who

referred her to specialists, who ordered flu shots, a mammogram and a colonoscopy. Doctors prescribed several pain killers, but never sent Correa to a pain specialist.

Dr. Michael Bernstein, a physician with Kaiser Permanente, defended Correa's care, but he acknowledged that doctors did not communicate well with her and should have referred her to pain specialists.

"I don't think people had given up on her, yet she may have felt that they did," said Bernstein, chairman of the ethics committee at the hospital where Correa was admitted.

Correa's suicide was particularly "unfortunate" and "frustrating," Bernstein said, because she had been scheduled to see a doctor in Fresno on Sept. 5 who could have referred her to Kaiser's pain clinic.

Correa canceled the appointment.

She went to Michigan on Sept. 6. The next day, she was dead.

Rebecca Badger, 39, of Goleta, Calif., was treated by two doctors for possible MS and received strong doses of morphine for pain relief from muscle spasms — a symptom of the disease.

Yet an autopsy showed that Badger had no signs of MS or any other physical disease.

Her primary doctor now acknowledges that Badger, an alcoholic and drug addict, may have had psychological problems and faked her illness.

In hindsight, "there was never any objective evidence for her complaints," said Dr. Johanna Meyer-Mitchell. "It could have been Munchausen."

Munchausen syndrome is a psychiatric disorder in which people fabricate symptoms to gain medical attention.

When she suspected MS, Meyer-Mitchell referred Badger in early 1988 to Dr. Michael Stein, a Walnut Creek, Calif., neurologist. After several tests, he declared "probable MS" and prescribed Valium. Later, Stein and Meyer-Mitchell wrote letters saying Badger had MS.

Badger also continued to see Meyer-Mitchell, who prescribed the antidepressant Prozac and psychological counseling. Badger saw a therapist once.

As Badger's complaints of pain escalated, Meyer-Mitchell prescribed liquid morphine in February 1995. She upped the dose in 1996, mailing the prescriptions to Badger's pharmacy when Badger moved to Goleta, several hours away.

Stein said he knew Badger was seeking Kevorkian's help, because he received a fax about her from Dr. Georges Reding, a psychiatrist who works with Kevorkian. But Stein said he didn't think Badger would go through with it.

Badger's daughter, Misty Nichols, now wonders if her mother had an unresolved psychiatric problem.

"At first I was so convinced that she had MS," Nichols said. "But now I think people who have a mental illness can manipulate people around them really good. Maybe that's what happened here."

Lois Hawes, 52, of Warren, made up her mind to die in May 1992, as soon as doctors told her that she had an advanced case of lung cancer that had spread to her brain. She was so determined to refuse all life-prolonging treatment that she even stopped doctors from testing to confirm the diagnosis.

But Kevorkian and Hawes' doctors concluded that a big reason behind her decision — beyond the fact Hawes had an advanced, aggressively growing cancer — was that the divorced, unemployed mother of four had no money and no medical insurance.

Some 40 million Americans have no medical coverage at any given moment. Medical ethics experts have speculated that poor and uninsured people might be particularly at risk if physician-assisted suicide were legalized.

Hawes, who was the fifth person to die with Kevorkian's help, may have been the first to bear out this theory about the economics of assisted death.

On Sept. 25, 1992, the night before Hawes died, she was seen by a Birmingham psychiatrist, Dr. Seymour Baxter, who reported his findings to Kevorkian on the phone at 9 p.m.

"Dr. Baxter was somewhat dismayed" that no biopsy had been done to confirm the cancer diagnosis, according to Kevorkian's extensive notes on the conversation.

"He felt that part of the reason why Lois had ... refused any surgical, X-ray or chemotherapy was her lack of sufficient money and lack of medical insurance," Kevorkian wrote, according to notes contained in a police file from the Hawes death investigation.

While Kevorkian and Baxter both noted other factors influencing Hawes' decision to die, Kevorkian wrote, referring to her inability to pay for extensive medical care, "I agreed with Dr. Baxter's assessment, and we both deplored the current state of medical service in this country which is responsible for such human tragedy."

The next day at around 11 a.m., Kevorkian provided Hawes with carbon monoxide to kill herself.

Nancy DeSoto, 55, of Lansing, Ill., noticed that her arms were sore about the time her legs began to drag in January 1995.

A doctor told her it was just arthritis and prescribed an ointment. She sought a second opinion from another doctor, who said the same thing.

Believing she'd had a stroke, DeSoto sought a third opinion from an internist near her Indiana summer home. Her family said he ran weekly tests for six months, $40,000 worth, to conclude that DeSoto had a pinched nerve in her neck.

DeSoto remained skeptical as her physical condition continued to deteriorate.

"Not knowing what was wrong was the worst part about it," said her eldest daughter, Rhonda Reitveld.

Soon she could walk only with a cane. With her husband, Joe, she holed up in a library, reading books and trying to figure out what was wrong.

In November 1995, a specialist at Northwestern University confirmed the couple's theory of ALS.

"She was so frustrated," said Reitveld. "How could they do so many tests and not know?"

Reitveld remembers the physician at Northwestern telling her that doctors "generally conduct thousands of dollars worth of tests so they don't have to tell you you're going to die."

DeSoto wrote Kevorkian last spring. She asked him to help her die after her youngest daughter, who was getting married in September, returned from her honeymoon.

DeSoto died Oct. 17.

Judith Curren, 42, of Pembroke, Mass., had felt sick and tired since she was 21, living with a disease that remains misunderstood and misdiagnosed.

Chronic Fatigue Syndrome can't be detected with a test. Instead, a diagnosis is based on numerous, persistent symptoms, such as headaches, sleep problems, muscle and joint pain and difficulty concentrating.

There are no effective treatments, although Curren tried many — psychotherapy, electroshock, steroid drugs, herbs and magnesium injections. Some unconventional combinations of drugs helped reduce her symptoms, but nothing worked for very long, said her husband, Frank.

Curren, a registered nurse with two young daughters, had a severe case of Chronic Fatigue Syndrome. Her symptoms slowly progressed for 20 years, until she was bedridden and obese, unable to care for her children or make most doctors' appointments, unless she pepped herself up with amphetamines, said her husband, Dr. Franklin Curren, a Pembroke, Mass., psychiatrist.

"She wasn't out of the house a day of her life in last five years without taking stimulants," he said.

Her health problems included an adrenal insufficiency; adult-onset asthma; winter depression, or Seasonal Affective Disorder, and Raynaud's disease, a circulation problem that can make fingertips numb in cold weather.

She had severe problems with narcolepsy, a sleep disorder that caused her to have attacks of deep sleep, sometimes for a day and a half. When awakened, she'd be semi-comatose and irritable, her husband said. She suffered from frequent high fevers, sweated profusely and had periodic bouts of intractable vomiting.

"Her most debilitating symptoms were cognitive ones," her husband said. "She couldn't think, couldn't keep thoughts straight on bad days.

"She couldn't read any more. The words would swim on the page. She had the same book under her pillow for nine months. She couldn't watch TV; it gave her migraines. She couldn't listen to music; it would drive her crazy."

Curren said his wife saw dozens of doctors over the years, some good, some bad. He said one enraged her during a 1992 hospitalization by describing Chronic Fatigue Syndrome as "a diagnosis for neurotic women."

"She basically quit at that point," Curren said. "She was so demoralized."

Soon, Judith Curren contacted Kevorkian. It took her more than four years to convince Kevorkian to take her case, mostly because she had been misdiagnosed as depressed, her husband said.

But by June 1996, Kevorkian called and agreed to help Curren end her life, her husband said. Just a few months earlier, her doctors had indicated her case was hopeless.

In March 1996, Dr. George Cuchural Jr., an infectious diseases specialist who became her primary care doctor, recommended that Judith Curren be placed in a nursing home.

Another Curren physician, Dr. David Bell, a nationally recognized chronic fatigue expert, concluded: "Because of the severity of her symptoms, I do not have any treatment suggestions that are likely to cause her resolution of her illness."

Frank Curren acknowledges, "There's nothing they could have done" to help his wife, who was mainly bedridden and, at 5 feet 1, weighed 260 pounds when she died. "They tried everything.

"In her mind she wasn't committing suicide," Curren said. "She was treating her illness. It was her way to end her misery."

He faults the medical establishment in part for not committing more money to research and understanding of Chronic Fatigue Syndrome.

Tom Skinner, a spokesman at the federal Centers for Disease Control and Prevention, said the agency has devoted millions of dollars to the syndrome for more than a decade.

"It's not something we take lightly," he said.

Nicholas Loving, 27, of Phoenix, started to notice in 1993 that he couldn't run as fast or jump as high on the basketball court. That fall, he developed a limp that really scared him.

With no primary care doctor or health insurance, his mother, Carol, took him to the emergency room of St. Joseph Hospital in Phoenix. Loving was admitted and doctors ran tests for five days.

Finally, Carol Loving recalled, a doctor appeared in Nicholas Loving's room and bluntly told him: "What you have used to be called Lou Gehrig's disease — and you're going to die from this."

She said her son was so stunned, he couldn't think of any questions to ask. Carol Loving said the doctor told Nicholas there was nothing the medical profession could do for him and left the room, saying, "You can go home."

Angry about the way the news had been dropped on her son, Carol Loving demanded to see a doctor. All she said she learned from that meeting was that ALS "could go on for two years or five years or 15 or 20 years. We just don't know."

In fact, half the people with ALS die within three years of diagnosis.

"These doctors we were talking to, they wouldn't give us a straight answer," said Carol Loving. "They lied to us.

"Dr. Kevorkian told us that the younger you are when you get this disease, the more accelerated the disease becomes," Loving said. "Dr. Kevorkian knew all about it."

The Lovings' relationship with doctors deteriorated as they went through an experimental treatment program and hospice care.

Nicholas Loving entered a program for ALS patients at the Barrow Neurological Institute, an affiliate of St. Joseph Hospital, but dropped out because he found the daily exercise regimen too exhausting.

Carol Loving said the doctor in charge told her son: "If you're not in the program, then I'm not your doctor any more. Don't call on me for anything."

She said her son spent his final months smoking marijuana to relieve his pain and planning his death.

Robin Cook, spokeswoman for Mercy Health Arizona, owner of St. Joseph Hospital and Barrow Neurological Institute, disputed Loving's account.

She said Nicholas Loving missed at least two appointments in an experimental drug and therapy program at Barrow, and that the staff had to contact him to learn that he was withdrawing.

"We're a Catholic institution," Cook said. "Our primary focus is to maintain a high quality of care. ... Nothing is more important to us.

"This is the first time I heard about this."

John Evans of Royal Oak got on his bike one warm day in January 1995 and was astonished that he couldn't make it to the corner, two houses away. He knew he'd been slowing down, but it worried him to be so exhausted by simple activities.

A month later, Evans learned he had less than six months to live due to pulmonary fibrosis, an incurable lung disease.

His wife, Jan Evans-Tiller, recalled how dejected her husband was after a visit to Dr. Robert Begle, medical director of medical critical care at William Beaumont Hospital. Begle had prescribed oxygen to help Evans breathe, but was leery of prescribing sleeping pills for him.

"I really want to get hold of Kevorkian," Evans told his wife. He said Begle had informed him that in two to six months, "I will either suffocate or I will go into cardiac arrest.

"I would like not to do either of those things, if it's possible," Evans said. "Those are not nice ways to die."

In three months, Evans, 78, was dead, opting to commit suicide with Kevorkian's help.

Begle, who had only seen Evans twice and not in the past three months, told police he would sign a death certificate listing natural causes. But he neither examined the body nor asked any questions of Evans' family.

Begle called filling out the death certificate "standard practice." An autopsy confirmed death by carbon monoxide poisoning. Begle declined to discuss his care of Evans, saying it would be "inappropriate for me to discuss confidential patient matters."

Jack Miller, 53, was dying of lung cancer that had spread to his bones. He was under the care of Hospice of Southeastern Michigan at his girlfriend's mobile home in Huron Township, near Belleville.

The girlfriend, Cynthia Coffey, said Miller was in great pain, but no one ever tried a morphine patch for him until Kevorkian suggested it.

Dr. John Finn, hospice medical director, said he can't recall who suggested the patch, but he acknowledged difficulty in relieving Miller's suffering.

"There were some impediments to effective pain management that were out of our control," he said, such as Miller not always following directions about taking medicine.

"He wasn't open to a lot of suggestions we would have," he said.
Miller's bigger problem was that he needed 24-hour care, but was reluctant to leave his home, Finn said.
He said hospice workers were horrified to learn of Miller's death. Later, they found out that a hospice staffer caring for Miller one day had intercepted a call from Kevorkian, and reported the incident to a social worker, but it was never relayed further.

Ronald Mansur, 54, of Birmingham, who also had lung cancer that had spread to his bones, never felt like a doctor listened to him until Kevorkian, said his sister, Jan Wilcox.
She said he thought his doctor at Henry Ford Hospital in Detroit had relegated him to the care of the nursing staff without giving him an idea of how long he might expect to live and how he would die.
Wilcox said Kevorkian encouraged Mansur to have chemotherapy treatment and a morphine pump for pain relief.
A hospital spokeswoman said Dr. Robert Chapman, Mansur's cancer doctor there, couldn't talk about him without permission from Mansur's daughter, who declined to give it.
Mansur died May 16, 1993.

— *Patricia Anstett*

THE MAJOR PROBLEMS

Many of the people who sought help dying from Dr. Jack Kevorkian had encountered problems with the medical profession. These were the most common or glaring:

- Doctors who provided only cursory care — exams, tests, prescriptions but little else, including compassion or discussion of important personal issues.
- Misdiagnosis.
- Poor case management — patients bounced from specialist to specialist.
- Inadequate pain management.
- Overlooking or ignoring mental health issues such as depression and substance abuse.
- Stereotyping of female patients as people who imagine pain or illness.
- Inadequate referrals and case management for home-based medical needs.
- Lack of counseling after doctors were aware that a patient had contacted Kevorkian or was thinking about it.
- Lack of insurance or money for medical treatments and home-based care.

KEVORKIAN'S SUICIDES

Who were the 47 people who asked Jack Kevorkian to help them die? Free Press background investigations and interviews revealed this:

AVERAGE AGE:

58

Range
27-82

GENDER:

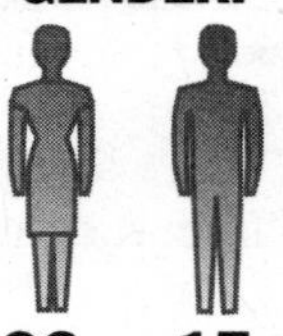

32 Women **15** Men

RACE: **46** white **1** Hispanic

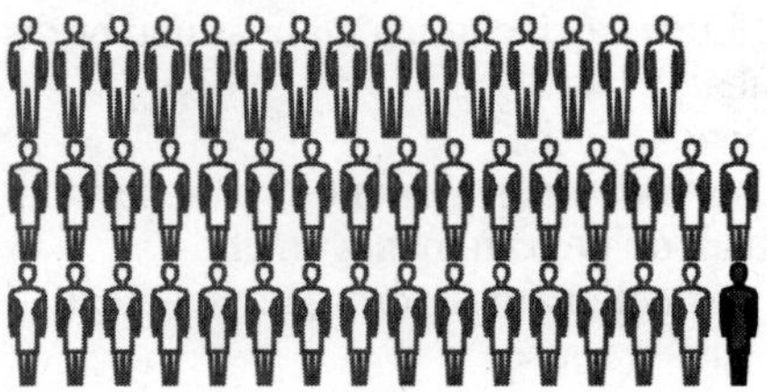

RELIGIOUS BACKGROUND:

13 Protestants **8** Roman Catholics **2** Jews

Many were not active in any religion at the time they died. Some were agnostics.

WORK:

25 disabled and could not work
14 retired
2 employed
3 unemployed
3 never worked outside the home
9 were or had been in health care
8 had worked in education
6 had worked in science or engineering

WHAT AILED THEM:

28 unable to walk
26 unable to go to the bathroom without help
18 incontinent
14 cancer
12 other disabilities ranging from blindness to inability to speak
11 depression
11 multiple sclerosis
11 had or complained of other ailments
9 ALS (Lou Gehrig's disease)
2 degenerative spinal cord diseases

SCHOOL:

14 had college degrees, including two with medical degrees, one with a law degree and four with master's degrees
10 had attended some college
12 were high school graduates
4 had not finished high school

The rest could not be determined.

FIRST TO FINAL MEETING:

At least **27** contacted Kevorkian themselves; at least **12** relied on an intermediary.

Kevorkian was in contact with **3** of them for more than a year, with **14** for less than a year, and with **11** for less than three months.

He was in touch with **4** of them for less than a month before they died, **1** less than two weeks and **1** for less than a day.

The rest could not be determined.

17 of them met Kevorkian for the first time on the day he helped them die. **11** others met with him twice and at least **7** had three or more sessions leading up to the final one.

The rest could not be determined.

OTHER CONTACTS:

At least **42** are known to have consulted with their families about their decision to die.

At least **9** consulted with a mental health professional.

At least **7** met with a religious figure.

HOME LIVES:

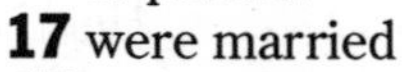

19 lived with a spouse or partner
17 were married
17 were divorced
14 lived with their children
14 lived alone
7 were single
6 were widowed single
6 lived with other family members
2 lived with paid help

DIAGNOSIS TO DEATH:

The average time from diagnosis of a major illness to a final meeting with Kevorkian was nearly **8** years.

The longest was nearly **50** years; the shortest was less than a month.

WHY SUICIDE?

36 had expressed fear of becoming dependent on others

34 were in chronic or cancer pain

At least **15** had been diagnosed with less than six months to live

13 had rejected any further medical treatment

At least **10** had tried suicide before

AFTERMATH:

41 of the 47 were cremated.

CONTROL AT THE END

The men and women who died with help from Dr. Jack Kevorkian were generally active, strong-willed and accustomed to being in control — of everything from the cut of their lawns to the color of their hair.

So when disease robbed them of control, they turned to Kevorkian to get it back — even if only for a final time.

You can always change your mind, Kevorkian tells people who ask for his help in committing suicide. It's going to be your choice, he says with an earnestness that is at once empowering and seductive.

By tying their fingers to the switch of one of his suicide machines, Kevorkian gives his patients what they want: a way to beat their diseases before the diseases beat them.

He gives them control.

"They get to a point," said Franklin Curren, a psychiatrist whose wife turned to Kevorkian after a long, debilitating illness, "where they say, 'I'm a master of very little, but this is one way I can be master of my final fate.' "

Shirley Cline, a 63-year-old cancer patient from Oceanside, Calif., was always in control, through two failed marriages and a series of feuds with family members. She was bossy with waiters and sent back food that wasn't prepared to her liking.

An active woman who loved to dance, she battled colon cancer until doctors performed an ileostomy — attaching a pouch to her side to collect bodily waste. Then she contacted Kevorkian.

Richard Faw, a 71-year-old psychiatrist from a small town in North Carolina who dyed his gray hair a coppery brown, also had a long bout with colon cancer, including numerous operations. But he continued to see patients during his fight and, despite great pain, lifted weights to stay in shape.

Losing strength, Faw became upset after being equipped with a colostomy bag that limited his activities.

"He was perfectly willing to do things for people," said a neighbor who tried unsuccessfully to get Faw signed up for Meals on Wheels deliveries, "but it was difficult for him to admit he needed help."

Barbara Ann Collins, 65, a researcher who had made a living studying the color perception of fish, was proud of her exacting, scientific mind.

"Her yellow flowers made a stick-straight line. Her house was meticulous," said a neighbor in Massachusetts.

When she developed ovarian cancer, Collins monitored her blood and devoured books on cancer. But the thought of constant medication and maybe even dying in a nursing home as her mother had was too much to endure.

"Bobbie Ann," the neighbor said, "liked to be in charge."

People close to those who committed suicide with Kevorkian's help say he gave options. In interviews, they described a period of euphoria after Kevorkian agreed to help.

Hugh Gale, 70, of Roseville, who once took pride in trimming and edging his lawn to perfection, spent the last years of his life housebound and tethered to an oxygen tank because of emphysema.

He was so upbeat following his first meeting with Kevorkian that his wife, Cheryl Gale, thought he had changed his mind about dying.

She said Kevorkian had the same impression.

"Well, Mr. Gale," she remembers Kevorkian saying the day her husband died, "I didn't think I'd ever hear from you again."

Cynthia Coffey said her fiance, Jack Miller, a 53-year-old tree trimmer from Huron Township, usually had trouble sleeping because of cancer pain, but didn't stir the night before Kevorkian helped him die.

In fact, Miller — who decided to commit suicide after doctors told him he would have to take his medications rectally — was in such high spirits the morning of his death, he joked that the carbon monoxide mask over his face made him look like a fighter pilot.

Linda Henslee, 48, of Beloit, Wis., had promised for years that she would take her own life before multiple sclerosis did.

She spent her final hours in an Oakland County motel room, celebrating with her two daughters. They ate chilled shrimp, chocolate eclairs and strawberries, drank champagne and scratched instant lottery tickets.

"We thought, 'Mom is in such a great mood. She's so ready to go. It feels like a birthday party,' " said daughter Dawn Henslee, 30, of Beloit. "So we went to the store and picked up all her favorite things."

Two nights before he died, Ronald Mansur, a 54-year-old real estate agent from Birmingham who wore a morphine pump to dull his pain from bone cancer, posed for a photograph. As his sister, Jan Wilcox, clicked the shutter, he stuck up his middle finger and laughed.

"If I could come back and talk to everybody," Mansur said to Wilcox, "I would tell them, 'You try this and see what you would do.' "

A year out of prison where he had served time for Medicaid fraud, Mansur — a sharp dresser who reveled in putting together business deals — was supposed to be starting his life anew when he was diagnosed with cancer. He was engaged to be married for the third time. He was poised to take over the family real estate business.

"He couldn't fulfill his hopes, the dreams that everybody has," said Wilcox. "His anger was 'I got cheated.'

"The only thing he could control was what time he would eat and what he would eat or what TV thing he would watch. He didn't make any decisions on what he could wear. I mean, Jesus!"

For people like Mansur, choosing Kevorkian is a way to avenge everything that seems to keep them from regaining control — including the medical profession, an institution for which many of Kevorkian's clients and their families expressed little respect.

"I do not want to be an object to generate profit for those medical entities who will prolong my life against my wishes when I am no longer able to protest," said Isabel Correa, a 60-year-old Californian with a spinal tumor who came to Michigan to die with Kevorkian's help.

Miller, who was the first man on Kevorkian's list of assisted suicides, "just started going from doctor to doctor," said Coffey. "They didn't have any answers. ... There's more doctor in Dr. K's little pinkie than all of the doctors put together. He just came across as caring."

In Kevorkian, patients find someone who is not afraid of losing a medical license; his was revoked years ago. They find someone who is not afraid of police or prosecutors or granting a dying person's wish.

"Nobody is going to deny or contradict or argue. Not even the so-called law," Kevorkian told Thomas Hyde, a 30-year-old laborer and ex-convict from Novi who was disabled by Lou Gehrig's disease. "You're going to get what you want."

Stanley Ball usually did.

A former Michigan State University wrestler who nearly qualified for the 1932 Olympic team, Ball was an avid outdoorsman who skied until he was 80 and glaucoma stole his eyesight. Even after that, he continued to live alone, take clarinet lessons and, until his eyesight failed completely, walk the mile from his house into Leland for coffee.

Ball, 82, believed he'd lived a good, long life that would be marred in the end by pancreatic cancer.

"He said what he was afraid of was pain," said his daughter, Judy Brown, who lives near Washington. "I experienced him as being afraid of not being strong."

When Kevorkian asked if Mary Biernat, an Indiana woman Ball had never met, could also die at Ball's home, he answered without hesitation: "I've got a large house. Fill it to the rafters!"

"He believed in the rightness of assisted suicide," Brown said. "He wanted to maintain the integrity of his own life."

To that end, many men and women are willing to do just about anything for Kevorkian's assistance, although few have been as dedicated as Marguerite Tate, 70, of Auburn Hills.

Paralyzed by Lou Gehrig's disease, she made several appearances with Kevorkian before her death, proclaiming her intention to make use of his help.

In January 1992, Tate accompanied Kevorkian on "Donahue" and spoke of her frustration over a court order forbidding him from assisting in any more suicides.

The day after Catherine Andreyev, a 45-year-old, cancer-stricken real estate agent from Pennsylvania, became the sixth person to die in Kevorkian's presence, Tate asked a Free Press reporter, "I wonder what she had that I didn't?"

In December 1992, Tate, sitting in a wheelchair and barely able to speak, showed up at a press conference with Kevorkian, who pointed to her and said: "Marguerite Tate has no quality of life. Everyone can see that. Look at her!"

Twelve days later, shortly after scrawling "My family stinks" on a piece of paper, Tate died with Kevorkian's help. Through his attorney, Kevorkian said it was only a coincidence that her death came on the day that Gov. John Engler signed a law banning assisted suicide.

If Tate ever felt used by Kevorkian, she didn't complain.

In fact, patients seem to expect to be used by Kevorkian — just as they use him to get what they want.

"It was a trade-off," said the ex-husband of Elaine Goldbaum.

A 47-year-old multiple sclerosis patient from Southfield, Goldbaum decided to seek Kevorkian's help because she believed she would be guilty of a mortal sin if she committed suicide on her own.

"She got what she wanted, and Kevorkian got what he wanted," said the ex-husband, who spoke to the Free Press on the condition that his first name not be published.

"There were three areas that she felt were being served: one, her own self-interest; two, other people in her position would be helped, and three, Dr. Kevorkian."

The Rev. Ken Phifer says his longtime friend and parishioner Merian Frederick knew just what she was getting into with Kevorkian.

A 72-year-old Ann Arbor resident with Lou Gehrig's disease, she had spent much of her life quietly pursuing social causes such as a ban on nuclear weapons.

"I think that if Merian could have found ... a way to live longer without the fear of not being given what she wanted — release from her suffering —

when she wanted it, she would have chosen that," Phifer says.

"But given that those were options closed to her, she chose this. ... Because she was living the truth of the need to have this available for all people."

And in some instances, Kevorkian clients who have been publicized before their deaths seemed to enjoy the attention.

"Hey!" Jack Miller exclaimed one night as he saw Kevorkian on TV, "that's me they're talking about!"

Later, Coffey said: "For a guy that's never had nothing happen to him in his life, something like that, well, sure you're going to think about it! Everybody has their 5 minutes of fame!"

Rebecca Badger, 39, whose doctor thought she had multiple sclerosis until an autopsy revealed no sign of the disease, sat for a TV interview the day before she left California to meet Kevorkian in Michigan.

"I think the TV interview was two things," said Badger's best friend, Cecelia Moody. "It was pro-Kevorkian. She didn't want him to just be Dr. Death anymore. And it was to stress the lack of quality care."

John Evans, a socialist and former Unitarian minister who had spent a lifetime championing causes such as union organizing and draft resistance during the Vietnam war, wanted his death to be part of the public debate on assisted suicide.

When police mistakenly concluded he died of natural causes, Kevorkian attorney Geoffrey Fieger told Evans' wife, Jan Evans-Tiller, that she could leave it at that, if she wished.

Evans-Tiller said no, explaining that her husband wanted his death to be "a political statement about what he thought was right and what should be the right of every person."

Evans-Tiller also said her husband knew "his death would be an important one because he had been a minister. So he knew what he was doing."

But he needed Kevorkian to do it.

— Georgea Kovanis

NATIONAL COMPARISON

More than 30,000 Americans commit suicide each year. As with the people who have sought help from Dr. Jack Kevorkian, serious, painful illness is often a factor. But there are significant differences, too, between what is known about the typical American suicide, and what is known about the people helped to their deaths by Kevorkian.

GENDER:
Nationally, 81% of suicides are male; two-thirds of Kevorkian's have been women. Nationally, women attempt suicide three times more often than men attempt it.

AGE: Nationally, the suicide rate is highest among people over age 65, who account for 19 percent of all such deaths. The average age for people aided by Kevorkian is 58, ranging from 27 to 82.

RACE:
Nationally, 90% of suicides are white people, 7% are black, 3% other. Of the 47 people known to have died with Kevorkian's help, the only non-white was a Hispanic woman.

OCCUPATION:
Nationally, the highest suicide rates are found among those who work in health care, law enforcement and agriculture. While most of the 47 people aided by Kevorkian were disabled or retired, eight had backgrounds in education, nine in health care and six in science or engineering.

Sources: Free Press research, National Center for Health Statistics, National Institute for Occupational Safety and Health, and Dr. Alan Berman, American Association of Suicidology

MARRIAGE:
Nationally, suicide is more than twice as common among widowed, divorced or single people than among married people. Of the 47 people aided by Kevorkian, only 17 were married when they died.

MENTAL HEALTH:
Nationally, mental health is considered the most important factor for suicide, with more than 90 percent of suicides suffering from conditions such as depression, schizophrenia or substance abuse. Among people aided by Kevorkian, less than a third had such conditions.

RECENT TROUBLES:
Nationally, risk factors for suicide include divorce, separation, unemployment, living alone and grieving. Among the 47 people aided by Kevorkian, 12 had such problems within a year before they died, and another 22 within five years of their suicide.

METHOD:
Nationally, more than 60 percent of men who kill themselves use a gun; about a third of women do. The second most common method for both is poisoning. Kevorkian helped all 47 of his suicides poison themselves, either with carbon monoxide gas, a lethal injection of drugs or both.

ON THE CHEAP

Jeanne Bogen stared in disbelief at the two heads silhouetted in the car in front of her. As the driver made a wide turn, she saw his passenger topple out of sight.

"Bette fell forward," Bogen recalled, "and there was Dr. Kevorkian, swerving down the road and struggling to get Bette's body upright again."

Bette was Bette Lou Hamilton, Bogen's best friend. A short time earlier, Hamilton had committed suicide with the help of Dr. Jack Kevorkian in a $69-a-night Telegraph Road motel room.

Now, Bogen was riding with Kevorkian helper Neal Nicol, following Dr. Death north toward Pontiac Osteopathic Hospital.

Kevorkian parked a few blocks from the hospital. With Nicol's help, he pulled a rickety wheelchair from the back seat of his car and lifted Hamilton's body into it. Then Kevorkian told Bogen she would be delivering the corpse.

Bogen didn't question it. She began pushing. "My heart was just pounding," she said.

Hamilton, who had a rare spinal disorder, weighed just 117 pounds, but Bogen learned how awkward and unwieldy a dead body can be as the corpse began slipping from the chair.

"I almost lost Bette right there, trying to wheel her in," she said.

As she struggled toward the emergency room doors, Bogen remembers, Kevorkian called to her:

"Don't forget to get the wheelchair back."

Bogen remembers thinking that if her friend were alive, "she would be laughing her head off."

From the cars and equipment he uses to the settings he chooses, Kevorkian's assisted suicides reflect the way he lives — frugal to a fault. In combination with the usual secrecy of his proceedings, the result is sometimes scenes of black humor, as when Bogen saw her friend's corpse flopping, or nearly lost her from the wheelchair.

Before becoming famous, Kevorkian lived in a one-bedroom apartment above a store in downtown Royal Oak. He has since moved into a lakefront house in West Bloomfield Township owned by his lawyer, Geoffrey Fieger.

But Kevorkian, a retired pathologist, still prides himself on saving a buck, shopping at flea markets and thrift stores.

"He's not wasteful," said longtime Kevorkian associate Janet Good. "He's very proud of the fact that he finds bargains. He loves to tell me how much he saved finding something he needs at the Salvation Army."

That would include the baby-blue cardigan Kevorkian wore at several deaths and through three trials. He bought the 100-percent Orlon sweater at the Salvation Army thrift store in Royal Oak in 1989 for $1.50. The sweater sold at a charity auction last summer for $4,200.

Although Kevorkian does not charge a fee for his suicide services, he is frugal by nature, not necessity, said Good.

"I'm not aware of all his finances, but I know he loves to save money. ... He doesn't really need to save money."

Kevorkian's frugality may be partly to blame for his lingering trouble with the law.

Routinely videotaping interviews with people before helping them die, he will put several interviews on one tape.

When Bloomfield Township police raided a hotel room where he was meeting with a woman Sept. 6, they seized several of Kevorkian's items — including a videotape of interviews.

One woman on the tape identified herelf as Loretta Peabody of Ionia, a 54-year-old woman with multiple sclerosis whose death Aug. 30 had been ruled natural. After an investigation, an Ionia County grand jury indicted Kevorkian and Good for assisting in Peabody's suicide.

Kevorkian, who has been acquitted three times of similar charges, is scheduled for trial in Ionia in late spring.

Ten of Kevorkian's assisted suicides died in their own homes. But the rest generally died in makeshift or spartan accommodations.

"We're doing this under cloak-and-dagger methods and it's very hard," Good said. "We have to slip in and out of places, trying not to be detected."

Sherry Ann Miller and Marjorie Wantz, both from Michigan, died together in the fall of 1991 in an Oakland County cabin intended to get young campers closer to nature. A favorite with Cub Scout troops, the $35-a-day cabin was bare of furnishings and lacked electricity and indoor plumbing.

Erika Garcellano of Merriam, a Kansas City suburb, who died in June 1995, was the only Kevorkian suicide known to have died at a short-lived clinic that he set up in a former hardware store on Dixie Highway in northwest Oakland County's Springfield Township. The clinic was furnished with two folding chairs, a metal table and an old bunk bed set in an area partitioned by a blanket and a printed bedsheet. A matching sheet covered a window.

At least a half dozen people died at the modest, two-story home of Kevorkian helper Neal Nicol, in Waterford Township just north of the runway at Oakland County International Airport.

Nicol put a sign reading "Police Entrance" over his front door after repeated investigations into assisted suicides in the home.

Rebecca Badger of California died last July at the Concorde Inn in Waterford Township, where rooms rent for $69 a night. Judith Curren of Massachusetts, who died in August, was registered at the same hotel, as was the son-in-law who brought Louise Siebens from Texas to die in Michigan last summer.

Kevorkian delivered those bodies to hospitals without disclosing where the deaths occurred.

In October, police broke up a meeting between Kevorkian and Nancy DeSoto of Illinois at the Dunes Motel on Woodward in Royal Oak. Rooms there rent for $25 a day and a paper sign posted on the Plexiglas-encased counter reminds customers that city ordinance prohibits by-the-hour rentals.

Good said Kevorkian used the Dunes Motel for consultations, but "no one I know has ever stayed there."

Shirley Cline of California, who died with Kevorkian's help last summer, was used to the better things in life. But, like Hamilton, she died in a room at the Quality Inn on Telegraph Road in Bloomfield Township, where a double costs $69 a night and the faded floral bedspread matches the drapes.

Good said some of Kevorkian's clients stayed in nice hotels, but Kevorkian would usually suggest his own favorites: Red Roof Inn, the Quality Inn or "that one where they leave the light on for you."

Kevorkian once refused to stay at a hotel because it was too nice, says Michael Rowady, a University of Detroit Mercy law student who clerks for Kevorkian's lawyer Geoffrey Fieger.

Because Kevorkian fears airplanes, Rowady was assigned last July to drive him to Washington, D.C., for an appearance at the National Press Club.

Arriving at the Embassy Suites Hotel, where a room cost about $170 a night, Kevorkian refused to go inside. "I'm not going into that nice hotel," Rowady recalls him saying. Kevorkian insisted he would sleep in the car.

Kevorkian was finally cajoled into bunking at the Embassy as Rowady's roomate, the clerk said.

Said Good, "That's why he and my husband get along so well. They both love to save money."

Kevorkian is also sparing with the means he uses for assisted suicide — but apparently more from necessity than choice. No longer a licensed physician in Michigan, Kevorkian has trouble getting the necessary drugs or carbon monoxide.

With Cline, he used so little Seconal to put her to sleep that her son, Dennis Garling, who was there, figures Cline spent the last 15 minutes of her life in mounting irritation, complaining: "Nothing's happening.

Nothing's happening. It's not working."

Garling said it appeared Kevorkian was trying to "stretch the meds."

Catherine Andreyev, a Pennsylvania woman who died in November 1992 at Nicol's home, took several deep breaths of carbon monoxide before saying, through a mask, "it's not working."

"Keep trying," said Kevorkian. "Of course it will work."

More minutes passed, more deep breaths, and Andreyev was still very much alert — and increasingly distraught. Kevorkian and Nicol checked the canister of gas.

The mixture was too weak. It wasn't lethal.

"They did this on purpose!" Kevorkian exclaimed angrily, thinking the carbon monoxide company had sabotaged him.

"Poor Catherine was just struggling to breathe, because every breath was so painful," said Leslie DiPietro, who witnessed her friend's death. "She was weeping; we all were."

Kevorkian told Andreyev he had another canister and he was prepared to proceed, but added, "You can stop this now."

Andreyev said she would go on. The second tank was hooked up, and it worked.

For Hamilton, Kevorkian used his suicide machine — an assemblage of bottles and tubes with a switch enabling people to deliver their own, deadly intravenous cocktail.

True to form, "the whole thing looked like something Dr. Kevorkian had made in his garage with an Erector set," Bogen said.

When Rebecca Badger died, the machine wasn't working right. She pulled a string to begin the flow of drugs, but instead of drifting off to sleep, "she got a burning sensation in her arm and she kept saying, "Ow. It hurts. It hurts," recalled her daughter, Christy. "They had to fix it. It took a couple minutes, but she finally went to sleep."

Perhaps the best example of Kevorkian's economy and efficiency is the five occasions when he has assisted in two suicides at once.

"We do doubles to save time and medication and to facilitate the arrangements," said Good.

— *Kate McKee*

CHEAP ROOMS

Here is a transcript of a portion of a telephone conversation between Dr. Jack Kevorkian and Bill Wantz on the day before Kevorkian helped Wantz's wife, Marjorie, commit suicide in a cabin in Oakland County in 1991. Wantz taped the call.

Wantz: What about the rent?
Kevorkian: Rent for the cabin?
Wantz: Yeah.
Kevorkian: Well, I don't know, I think it's $35 ...
Wantz: Oh, I don't mean that, I mean somebody's got to rent it.
Kevorkian: What, the cabin?
Wantz: Yeah, tomorrow.
Kevorkian: Yeah, uh, it's been reserved. My sister called. It's been reserved for you and Marge.

After discussing travel directions, they talk about nearby motels where the couple, from Sodus in Berrien County, can spend the night before she dies.

Kevorkian: There are three motels there.
Wantz: Mm Hmm.
Kevorkian: ... But Days Inn is too expensive.
Wantz: Well, that ... that isn't the point, that we, couple dollars ...
Kevorkian: No, it's not a couple. It's $67 for a double.
Wantz: I see.
Kevorkian: Uh, but, uh, Red Roof, I think is $36.
Wantz: Uh huh.
Kevorkian: For a double. And there's also a, uh, Super 8 motel there. You can see all three ... the cheapest and the two best ones are both about $36 or $37. Red Roof ...
Wantz: Yeah.
Kevorkian: ... and Super 8.
Wantz: Yeah, OK.
Kevorkian: For a double.
Wantz: OK.
Kevorkian: You can see both of them from the freeway. ... Get off on Little Mack and go north.
Wantz: Okey-dokey.

Wantz puts his wife on the phone. She tells Kevorkian she is in considerable pain. Then Wantz is back on the line.

Wantz: Yeah, doc?
Kevorkian: Bill.
Wantz: (wife speaking in background) You want ... she wants to know if you want me to bring a rubber mallet? That would do better to relax her.
Kevorkian: (laughs) That's ...
Wantz: See, that's about the only way you'll relax her.
Kevorkian: She hasn't lost her sense of humor, despite the pain.

BLUNT AND SHY

The slight, gray-haired man marched into the offices of the Daily Tribune of Royal Oak one spring day in 1990, introduced himself as a retired pathologist and said he wanted to place this ad:

"Jack Kevorkian, M.D. Bioethics and Obitiatry. Special death counseling. By appointment only."

Showing a photograph of a glass-and-tubing contraption he'd made from $30 worth of scrap parts, Kevorkian said it was a suicide machine, and announced: "I want to help people who want to end their lives."

The ad saleswoman hesitated, then suggested he see Ben Burns, the editor and publisher. Burns refused to take Kevorkian's ad.

"He was cross," said Burns, now a journalism professor at Wayne State University. "But I told him I had no idea who would buy it and use it. What if a depressed teenager responded?"

Kevorkian called Burns a censor and walked out of the office in a huff.

Not much of a start for a man who would, over the next few months, become a household name across America — the subject of magazine covers, talk shows and countless jokes on late-night TV.

As Kevorkian helped almost four dozen people end their lives over the next seven years, starved himself in jail and walked away free from three criminal trials, he developed a love-hate relationship with the news media, stoked by his outrageous and irascible attorney, Geoffrey Fieger.

At first, however, Kevorkian was just a curiosity. His initial attempts at advertising in Detroit-area papers and in medical journals were rebuffed, and only a few publications, including the Free Press, did short stories about the maverick pathologist.

One of those briefs, in Newsweek magazine, caught the eye of Ronald Adkins in Portland, Ore.

Adkins took Kevorkian seriously. In June 1990, he brought his wife, Janet, to Michigan to die. A former teacher diagnosed with Alzheimer's disease, she became the first person to use his machine — and vaulted Kevorkian into a national spotlight.

"Death with Dignity?" teased Newsweek's cover.

"As Memory and Music Faded, Oregon Woman Chose Death" said the New York Times in a front-page story about Adkins' last days.

Kevorkian said he never wanted publicity, but the week after Adkins' death he ran the news and talk show gamut — from "Nightline" and "Good Morning America" to "Geraldo."

As Kevorkian became the lightning rod for a national debate on the right to die, police investigating Adkins' death said they felt pressured to conclude something — even though Michigan law on assisted suicide was murky.

"We got a call for a 'physician-assisted suicide.' We had never heard of such a thing," said Lt. David Haire, one of two Michigan State Police detectives who worked full-time for six months on the Adkins case. "We were in new territory."

Ultimately, Kevorkian was charged with murder. He needed a lawyer.

Relying on news accounts of a bold attorney who had begun moving furniture out of a hospital as payment for a malpractice claim, Kevorkian called Fieger.

The murder charge in Oakland County was quickly dismissed, and the short, wiry doctor and the big, brash lawyer remained together in the public eye through suicide after suicide.

In addition to the police investigation, another result of all the attention was more scrutiny of Kevorkian and the people who came to him for help, much of it unfavorable to Kevorkian. Even Derek Humphry, director of the Hemlock Society, a national right-to-die organization, decided Kevorkian was "too obsessed, too fanatical, in his interest in death and suicide, to offer direction for the nation."

In 1991 year-end editorials, newspapers began to chastise Kevorkian for the standards he used to determine who received his help.

By spring 1992, Kevorkian appeared disheartened by the criticism. In a videotape he made with Susan Williams before her death, he said: "I don't like to talk to news people anymore. They slant it negatively."

A few months later, he told the family of another woman that he wasn't sure how much attention her death would get. "It seems to be less and less," he said.

In fact, Kevorkian-aided deaths were becoming routine to the news media, and to the police. For a September 1992 Kevorkian-assisted suicide in Waterford Township, police compiled a voluminous record that included medical reports, Kevorkian's notes and two videotapes. Less than five months later, when Kevorkian helped two people die on the same day in Waterford, the police report was about 400 words.

By June 1996, the Pontiac police's follow-up investigation of Ruth Neuman's suicide amounted to a phone call to Fieger's office. When they received a "no comment" from him, they quickly closed the case. A note on the police report added: "Attorney Fieger stated that he appreciated how the Police Dept. was handling the suicide."

Pontiac police officers joked that Kevorkian was dropping off bodies with such frequency that they would open an express checkout lane for him.

As Kevorkian's activity became commonplace, he became a celebrity, a name that needed no explanation as a punch line or reference in one of talk-show host David Letterman's Top 10 lists. His ghoulish paintings sold for $150 to $200 apiece at the Ariana Gallery in Royal Oak.

In the summer of 1994, Kevorkian had received the Humanist Hero award from the American Humanist Society. In a speech at its national meeting in Detroit, Kevorkian said the media had always taken a negative view of him. He said there was a conspiracy among organized religion, medicine and big money, and "the entire editorial policy of the country is one side."

Fieger helped create a furor in August 1995 when he advised Kevorkian to leave a woman's body in a car in the parking lot of a hospital to avoid the "circus-like atmosphere" and "body bag shots" that had accompanied earlier suicides. The body was left visible in the car surrounded by police crime-scene tape for hours, drawing news cameras and reigniting the debate over death with dignity.

By the summer of 1996, media interest, which had spiked during successive trials in Oakland County that ended with Kevorkian acquittals, waned again as Kevorkian helped 13 people die in a four-month span.

"News is a deviance, and when something becomes a regular occurrence it's often less newsworthy," said Mort Meisner, the news director for WJBK-TV (Channel 2) in Southfield. "Lately, it's been the same story with a different face."

Reporters generally accepted Fieger's summary version of medical conditions, blurred the distinction between chronic illness and terminal disease and fed the popular misconception that Kevorkian was only there for people facing inevitable and agonizing death.

For instance, the day after the body of a California woman, Rebecca Badger, was wheeled into a hospital in Royal Oak, virtually every news organization unquestioningly reported the Fieger-Kevorkian claim that she was suffering from multiple sclerosis.

When a detailed autopsy revealed no evidence of the disease, few media outlets took notice. Only when People magazine reported that Badger's physician had concluded her MS diagnosis was wrong did other media report the disturbing conclusion that Kevorkian had helped end the life of a woman with no anatomical illness.

"Fieger says, 'I paint a Picasso.' He paints this thing and it has absolutely nothing to do with the truth," said Detective Randy Armstrong of Bloomfield Township, where at least four Kevorkian-aided deaths occurred.

After police raided a meeting between Kevorkian and Isabel Correa in

September 1996 at a township motel, Fieger pushed her in her wheelchair back and forth in the parking lot, ranting about the police.

"Fieger is the P.T. Barnum of Michigan law," said professor Burns. "He puts on a big show and he's obviously good at it because the media puts it on the air, writes about it."

Kevorkian and Fieger were regarded as victors when Oakland County Prosecutor Richard Thompson, who twice brought Kevorkian to trial and planned to continue charging him, was defeated in his re-election bid last year.

The new prosecutor, David Gorcyca, declined to charge Kevorkian. But Badger's death raised questions that had not been asked in years about Kevorkian's standards and practices.

Newsweek's chatty "conventional wisdom" scorecard gave him a thumbs down at year's end, calling him a "creepy nut." A grand jury in Ionia County indicted him on charges of aiding Loretta Peabody's suicide there. He faces trial this spring.

So when two bodies were left recently at separate locations in Pontiac, with all the signs of a Kevorkian-assisted suicide — one was left in the same Volkswagen van where Janet Adkins died — it was not surprising that Kevorkian made no public statement acknowledging a role.

While his crusade for assisted suicide retains majority support in public opinion polls, the man known as Dr. Death appears to have gone low-profile.

But given his record, stay tuned.

— Ariana E. Cha

SOME KEVORKIAN CLIENTS AND LOVED ONES

PART THREE

THE PEOPLE

THE 47 WHO DIED

What did they have in common? They wanted to die. They wanted assurance that their decision would be final. Brief individual biographies follow.

1

June 4, 1990
Janet Elaine Adkins, 54, Portland, Ore.

A former college instructor on disability, she decided to commit suicide the day she was diagnosed with Alzheimer's disease. Dr. Jack Kevorkian agreed to help without ever speaking to her, only her husband. Adkins died of a lethal injection from Kevorkian's first suicide machine in his van at a campsite in Groveland Oaks County Park in rural Oakland County.

2

Oct. 23, 1991
Marjorie Lee Wantz, 58, Sodus, Mich.

A married former elementary school teaching assistant on disability, she had unexplained and untreatable vaginal pain. Wantz had a long history of depression and other psychiatric problems. She died by lethal injection in a double suicide in a cabin in Oakland County's Bald Mountain Recreation Area. An autopsy found nothing that could have caused the pain Wantz described.

3 **Oct. 23, 1991**
Sherry Ann Miller, 44, Roseville, Mich.

A former clerical worker on disability, she had multiple sclerosis and had moved back in with her parents because she could not take care of herself. Miller died from breathing carbon monoxide in the same Oakland County cabin where Wantz died a few minutes earlier. Divorced, she left behind two young children who lived with their father.

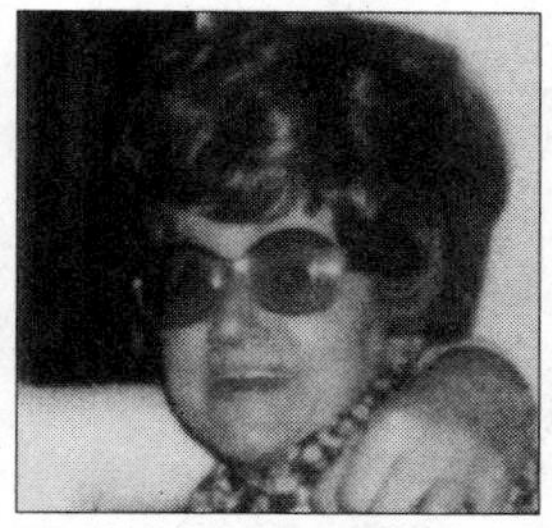

4 **May 15, 1992**
Susan Williams, 52, Clawson, Mich.

A homemaker, she died at home, with her family present. She inhaled carbon monoxide. Williams was legally blind, unable to walk due to multiple sclerosis, and had a long history of other medical problems, including cancer. She dictated a letter to Kevorkian, seeking his help, after seeing him on television. Kevorkian considered her the first client of his formal obitiatry practice.

5 **Sept. 26, 1992**
Lois Hawes, 52, Warren, Mich.

A divorced mother of four who looked after a brain-damaged son, Hawes had terminal cancer and died of carbon monoxide poisoning at the Waterford home of Kevorkian's assistant, Neal Nicol. She said she had watched her father and brother die of cancer, and did not want to undergo extraordinary treatment. Hawes was the first patient whose doctors cooperated with Kevorkian.

6

Nov. 23, 1992
Catherine Andreyev, 45,
Moon Township, Pa.

A single schoolteacher, Andreyev had cancer of the lungs, liver, lymphatic system and bones. She died of carbon monoxide poisoning at Nicol's home, less than a day after her first meeting with Kevorkian. One friend said the doctor exploited her at a weak moment; others said Andreyev was profoundly affected by her mother's agonizing death two years earlier.

7

Dec. 15, 1992
Marguerite Tate, 70,
Auburn Hills, Mich.

Tate was in the terminal stage of Lou Gehrig's disease when she died of carbon monoxide poisoning at her home, where Kevorkian assisted in another suicide the same day. Divorced and estranged from her only child, Tate championed Kevorkian's cause for a year before she died, appearing with him on talk shows and supporting him in court.

8

Dec. 15, 1992
Marcella Lawrence, 67,
Clinton Township, Mich.

A divorced nurse, Lawrence appeared at a press conference with Kevorkian 12 days before her death to denounce pending legislation to outlaw assisted suicide. She died at the home of Marguerite Tate on the day Gov. John Engler signed the bill into law. Lawrence suffered from heart disease, emphysema and arthritis but was not terminally ill. She died of carbon monoxide poisoning.

9

Jan. 20, 1993
Jack Miller, 53,
Huron Township, Mich.

A tree trimmer, Miller was the first male to seek Kevorkian's help. He suffered from cancer and emphysema, and feared going into a coma as his mother had done. He died from inhaling carbon monoxide at a trailer home he shared with his girlfriend. Miller's ex-wife and children learned of his death from a TV news report.

10

Feb. 4, 1993
Stanley Ball, 82,
Leland Township, Mich.

A widowed, retired county extension agent, Ball was part of a double assisted suicide with an Indiana woman at Ball's home on Lake Leelanau. The two met the night before. Ball was an Olympic prospect as a wrestler in 1932 and, although legally blind from glaucoma, skied until he was almost 80. He was diagnosed with cancer about a month before he died of carbon monoxide poisoning.

11

Feb. 4, 1993
Mary Biernat, 74,
Crown Point, Ind.

A seamstress and homemaker, Biernat died from inhaling carbon monoxide at the northern Michigan home of Stanley Ball, who also committed suicide that day. The two met the day before, and their families shared a duck dinner the night before the suicides. Biernat had breast cancer and walked with a cane, which she had tried, without explanation, to give away before coming to Michigan.

12 Feb. 8, 1993

Elaine Goldbaum, 47, Southfield, Mich.

A divorced mother who sold jewelry until her health forced her to quit in 1988, Goldbaum suffered from multiple sclerosis and required round-the-clock nursing care. In a letter to Kevorkian, Goldbaum said her loss of independence was "atrocious." She died of carbon monoxide poisoning in her Southfield apartment.

13 Feb. 15, 1993

Hugh Gale, 70, Roseville, Mich.

He was a merchant seaman and then a security guard until emphysema forced him to quit in 1985. Gale's wife overheard him asking God to "let me go" in 1991. Gale died of carbon monoxide poisoning at his home. The death became controversial when Kevorkian critics going through trash found papers indicating Gale had twice during the procedure changed his mind about dying.

14 Feb. 18, 1993

Jonathan Grenz, 44, Costa Mesa, Calif.

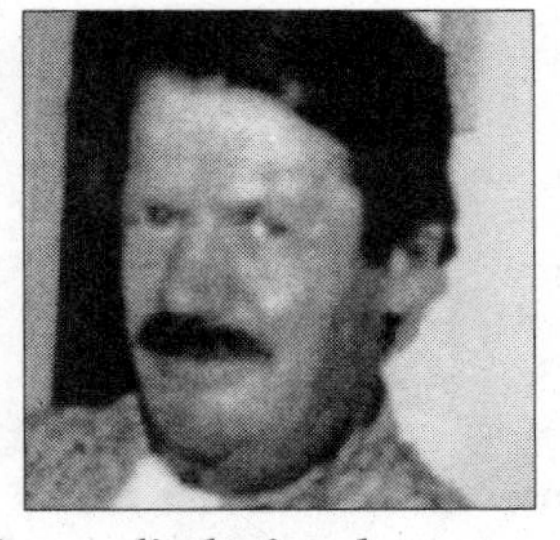

A single real estate agent, Grenz was terminally ill with throat cancer and had lost most of his tongue to surgery. His mother died of cancer shortly before he contacted Kevorkian. Grenz died of carbon monoxide poisoning in the Waterford Township home of Kevorkian's assistant, Nicol, one of two suicides there that day.

15 Feb. 18, 1993
Martha Ruwart, 40, San Diego, Calif.

A single computer programmer, Ruwart suffered from terminal duodenal and ovarian cancer. She had tried a number of alternative treatments, including shark's blood enemas, before asking a sister to contact Kevorkian four weeks before her death. Three sisters accompanied her to her final appointment, at the home of Kevorkian assistant Nicol. She inhaled carbon monoxide.

16 May 16, 1993
Ronald Mansur, 54, Birmingham, Mich.

Mansur worked in his family's Detroit real estate business, and died in a back room there of carbon monoxide poisoning. Mansur had cancer. He first contacted Kevorkian in November 1992, but Kevorkian persuaded him to continue chemotherapy and to try to control pain with a morphine pump. Mansur was divorced.

17 Aug. 4, 1993
Thomas Hyde, 30, Novi, Mich.

A divorced landscaper and carpenter, Hyde began talking about suicide shortly after he was diagnosed in August 1992 with ALS, or Lou Gehrig's disease. He rescheduled his appointment with Kevorkian so he could first cash a Social Security check. Hyde died from inhaling carbon monoxide in the back of Kevorkian's van.

18

Sept. 9, 1993
Donald O'Keefe, 73,
Redford Township, Mich.

A married, retired engineer, O'Keefe lived an active life until he developed bone cancer and a resulting intestinal disease that made his life miserable. He died from carbon monoxide poisoning at his home. O'Keefe begged Kevorkian to accept money for helping him, thrusting a wad of bills upon him. Kevorkian returned the money the next day.

19

Oct. 22, 1993
Merian Frederick, 72,
Ann Arbor, Mich.

A homemaker and political activist, Frederick suffered from ALS. She died from inhaling carbon monoxide in a room across the hall from Kevorkian's former second-floor apartment in downtown Royal Oak. Her death led to formation of Merian's Friends, a group trying to put a proposal on the 1998 Michigan ballot to legalize physician-assisted suicide.

20

Nov. 22, 1993
Ali Khalili, 61,
Oak Brook, Ill.

A married physician, Khalili chaired the department of rehabilitative medicine at Grant Hospital in Chicago and was an associate professor at the Northwestern University Medical School. He had bone cancer, and wore a morphine pump under his skin for pain control. Khalili inhaled carbon monoxide in the same Royal Oak apartment where Frederick died.

21 **Nov. 26, 1994**
Margaret Garrish, 72,
Royal Oak, Mich.

Crippled by arthritis and unable to work for years, Garrish had lost both legs to amputation. She died of carbon monoxide poisoning in her home with her husband present. Kevorkian had announced the previous March that he intended to help Garrish end her life unless a doctor came forward who could alleviate her chronic pain.

22 **May 8, 1995**
John Evans, 78,
Royal Oak, Mich.

A retired Unitarian Universalist minister, Evans suffered from a fatal lung disease. He died of carbon monoxide poisoning at home in his favorite chair. Authorities at first said it was natural causes, but Evans' widow told police what happened because her husband, a socialist and political activist, wanted to make a final statement in support of assisted suicide.

23 **May 12, 1995**
Nicholas Loving, 27,
Phoenix, Ariz.

A student, Loving was the youngest person to obtain Kevorkian's assistance with suicide. He suffered from ALS. Loving died from inhaling carbon monoxide at Nicol's Waterford Township home. He died listening to Pink Floyd and holding the hand of his mother, who has since become a crusader to legalize assisted suicide in Arizona.

24

June 26, 1995
Erika Garcellano, 60,
Kansas City, Mo.

A divorced nursing home aide who escaped war-ravaged Europe as a child, Garcellano was the only person to die at the Margo Janus Mercy Clinic, which Kevorkian set up in a former hardware store on Dixie Highway in Oakland County's Springfield Township. After her death, the building owners evicted Kevorkian. Garcellano had ALS. She had entered a nursing home a few months before her death.

25

Aug. 21, 1995
Esther Cohan, 46,
Skokie, Ill.

A single former secretary, Cohan was on disability due to multiple sclerosis. She died of carbon monoxide poisoning with her sister at her side. Kevorkian left her body in a car illegally parked just north of the emergency room entrance to William Beaumont Hospital in Royal Oak with a note that said "URGENT!" stuck on the windshield. The body was not discovered for two hours. (1967 photo)

26

Nov. 8, 1995
Patricia Cashman, 58,
San Marcos, Calif.

A world traveler, travel agent and freelance writer, Cashman lived alone in a mobile home park. After being diagnosed with cancer, she apparently feared the loss of her independence and wrote a letter asking for Kevorkian's assistance. Kevorkian left her body outside the Oakland County medical examiner's office in the same car in which Esther Cohan was found in August. She died from both carbon monoxide poisoning and lethal injection.

27

Jan. 29, 1996
Linda Henslee, 48,
Beloit, Wis.

A data communications manager for Georgia Pacific, Henslee was an outspoken advocate of right-to-die legislation. She wrote her own obituary, saying, "I do things my way — always have." Henslee had multiple sclerosis. She died from inhaling carbon monoxide while lying on a couch with her two adult daughters hugging her.

28

May 6, 1996
Austin Bastable, 53,
Windsor, Ontario

A toolmaker, Bastable was disabled by multiple sclerosis and had announced on the Internet his intention to die. He was married with two children. He was a crusader in Canada for right-to-die legislation, even accosting the prime minister one day to state his case. Bastable died from inhaling carbon monoxide at the home of Janet Good, a longtime Kevorkian supporter.

29

June 10, 1996
Ruth Neuman, 69,
Columbus, N.J.

A retired bus driver described as a "strong-willed woman," Neuman was diabetic, overweight and partially paralyzed by a stroke. Her husband had died the previous November. She died of carbon monoxide poisoning and was brought to a Pontiac hospital by her son three weeks before her death.

30 June 18, 1996
Lona Jones, 58,
Chester, Va.

A nurse, Jones suffered from occasional seizures after the surgical removal of a benign brain tumor. Around the time of her death, doctors said the tumor had reappeared, but her most recent treating physician said he was "shocked" by her suicide. Jones' body was wheeled into Pontiac Osteopathic Hospital by her husband, an official of the Virginia Department of Emergency Services. She died from both carbon monoxide poisoning and lethal injection.

31 June 20, 1996
Bette Lou Hamilton, 67,
Columbus, Ohio

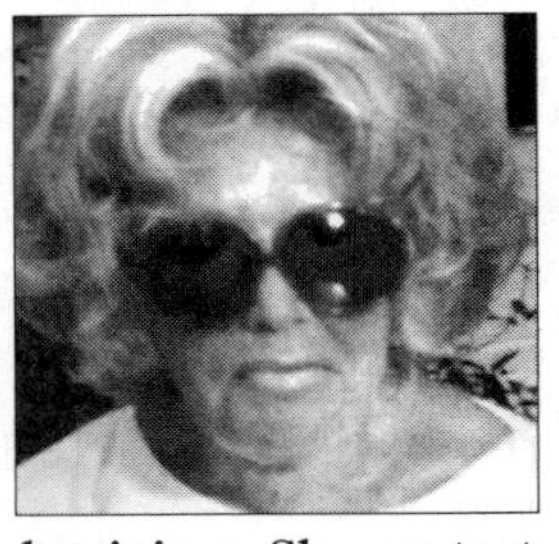

Hamilton was disabled by a spinal disorder and had little use of her hands as a result of a botched surgery in the 1950s, but she prided herself on being able to live independently in a condominium. She contacted Kevorkian as her condition deteriorated to a point where she was facing admission to a nursing home. Hamilton died of carbon monoxide poisoning in a motel room in Oakland County.

32 July 4, 1996
Shirley Cline, 63,
Oceanside, Calif.

A twice-divorced retired high school administrator, Cline had terminal bowel cancer spreading throughout her body. She died from a lethal injection less than three hours after meeting Kevorkian at a West Bloomfield Township motel. Cline was accompanied to Michigan by her son. Two weeks before her death, she donned an evening gown and went ballroom dancing.

33

July 9, 1996
Rebecca Badger, 39,
Goleta, Calif.

A single mother of two, Badger had a history of drug and alcohol abuse, and psychiatric and emotional problems. She was diagnosed with multiple sclerosis but an autopsy found no sign of the disease. Badger died from a lethal injection. California police believe her mother may have encouraged her to seek Kevorkian's help after assisting Badger in two failed suicide attempts.

34

Aug. 6, 1996
Elizabeth Mercz, 59,
Cincinnati, Ohio

A supervisor at a pillow factory, the twice-divorced Mercz was an immigrant from Hungary who had managed for most of her adult life to support herself and her three children. After she was diagnosed with ALS, one of her sons unsuccessfully tried to help her commit suicide, then contacted Kevorkian. She died from both carbon monoxide poisoning and lethal injection.

35

Aug. 15, 1996
Judith Curren, 42,
Pembroke, Mass.

A registered nurse who had not worked in 10 years, Curren suffered from a muscle disorder, depression and chronic fatigue syndrome. She complained of physical abuse by her husband, a psychiatrist. Others corroborated his story that he had fought to prevent her suicide. The couple was deeply in debt. Curren was also overweight and had been bedridden for up to two weeks at a time. She died of a lethal injection.

36 **Aug. 20, 1996**
Louise Siebens, 76,
McKinney, Texas

A homemaker, Siebens was an active member of her community and church and an avid golfer until she developed a rapidly progressing case of ALS, which in just a few months forced her into a nursing home. The Oakland County medical examiner believes she was too debilitated even to pull the switch that administered the lethal injection that Kevorkian arranged for her.

37 **Aug. 22, 1996**
Pat DiGangi, 66,
Long Island, N.Y.

A college history professor, DiGangi was diagnosed with multiple sclerosis in 1981 and by 1987 needed a wheelchair to get around. He talked of suicide for about two years but didn't arrange to come to Michigan to see Kevorkian until he became incontinent. His wife said DiGangi's great fear was "to live for a long time and keep getting worse." He died from a lethal injection.

38 **Aug. 22, 1996**
Patricia Smith, 40,
Lee's Summit, Mo.

A former nurse on disability because of multiple sclerosis, Smith left a 17-year-old daughter behind in Missouri when she came to Michigan to die. She was a Baptist who contacted Kevorkian only after her minister said killing herself would not bar her from entering heaven. Smith died of a lethal injection. Kevorkian delivered her body to Pontiac Osteopathic Hospital.

39

Aug. 30, 1996
Loretta Peabody, 54, Ionia, Mich.

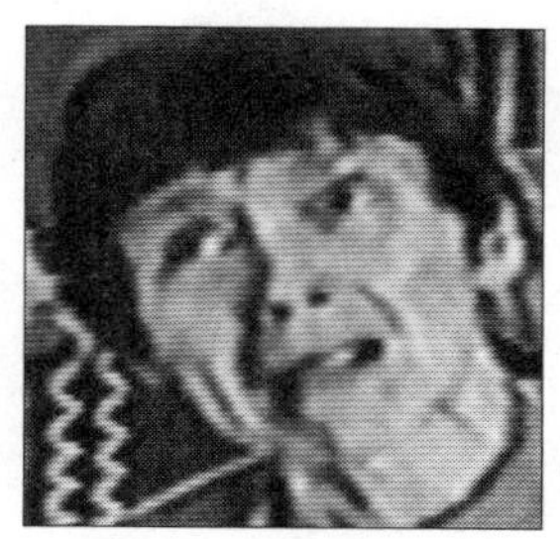

A homemaker, she lived with multiple sclerosis for 27 years before contacting Kevorkian. On a videotape she told him, "Thank God you are here." Peabody's death was listed as natural until the tape was found. In November, Kevorkian was indicted by an Ionia County grand jury on charges of helping Peabody kill herself. Her method of suicide is unknown.

40

Sept. 2, 1996
Jack Leatherman, 72, Knoxville, Tenn.

A retired engineer, Leatherman rejected medical treatment and contacted Kevorkian shortly after he was diagnosed with pancreatic cancer. A long-divorced father of three grown chldren, he made all his own arrangements with Kevorkian and died of a lethal injection in a room he had rented at the Holiday Inn Express in Birmingham.

41

Sept. 7, 1996
Isabel Correa, 60, Fresno, Calif.

A divorced packer at a sunflower and nut company, Correa was disabled by a worsening spinal cord condition. Correa, a Hispanic woman, is the only non-white to receive assistance from Kevorkian in committing suicide. Police interrupted her first meeting with Kevorkian by raiding the motel room where she was staying. She died the next day from inhaling carbon monoxide.

42 Sept. 29, 1996
Richard Faw, 71,
Wilson, N.C.

A psychiatrist, he was seeing patients at his home until a week before his death. He was fiercely independent, and had undergone surgery a dozen times since 1987 for colon cancer. Faw's daughters learned of his death on the Internet and a CNN newscast. He died from carbon monoxide poisoning. Faw was divorced and had been married three times.

43 Oct. 10, 1996
Wallace Spolar, 69,
Horizon City, Texas

A retired teacher, Spolar was said to be frustrated that multiple sclerosis and a bad heart had relegated him to getting around in a wheelchair. "His mind worked, his body didn't," one friend said. A World War II Navy veteran, Spolar was married with two grown daughters and two grandchildren. He died of carbon monoxide poisoning.

44 Oct. 17, 1996
Nancy DeSoto, 55,
Lansing, Ill.

A homemaker and retired florist, DeSoto had a rapidly advancing case of ALS and had spent nearly $40,000 on medical care. She arranged a date with Kevorkian to follow a daughter's wedding and honeymoon. Their initial meeting at a Royal Oak motel was interrupted by police who recognized Kevorkian's car. DeSoto died the next day from inhaling carbon monoxide.

45 **Oct. 23, 1996**
Barbara Ann Collins, 65,
North Falmouth, Mass.

A retired microbiologist, she had worked at the prestigious Marine Biological Lab in Woods Hole, Mass. Neighbors described her as a recluse who ventured outside only to tend obsessively to her flower garden. Collins contacted Kevorkian after she was diagnosed with ovarian cancer and had undergone several treatments. She died of a lethal injection.

46 **Feb. 2, 1997**
Lisa Lansing, 42,
Florham Park, N.J.

A single medical malpractice attorney, she complained for more than a decade of pain in her digestive system, although doctors in New Jersey could never determine that she had a medical problem. One physician said he refused to treat Lansing because she was interested mainly in obtaining prescription painkillers. She died from a lethal injection. Another woman left her body at Pontiac Osteopathic Hospital.

47 **Feb. 2, 1997**
Elaine Day, 79,
Newhall, Calif.

A widowed retired law office employee, Day was an avid golfer, dancer and swimmer who was being increasingly disabled by ALS. She detailed her suffering in a letter to the Los Angeles Daily News and expressed support for assisted suicide. Day died of a lethal injection. Her body was found in Kevorkian's Volkswagen van parked at the Oakland County medical examiner's office.

GABRIEL B. TAIT

KEVORKIAN GOES PUBLIC

This article appeared in the Free Press on March 18, 1990, almost three months before Jack Kevorkian's first assisted suicide.

The killing machine waits on the floor of his bedroom closet, next to a few cardboard cartons and a broken black-and-white television set.

The frame is scrap aluminum, leftover from one of Dr. Jack Kevorkian's earlier experiments. The motor came from a toy car. Plug it into a wall socket, punch it into your arm, press a button and five minutes later, you're dead.

It's painless, portable and legal. Kevorkian is certain it would work, if only someone would give it a whirl.

Applications are being accepted. Oppressed by a fatal disease, a severe handicap, a crippling deformity? Show him proper, compelling medical evidence that you should die, and Dr. Jack Kevorkian will help you kill yourself, free of charge.

"I don't care how it seems to healthy people," he says. "I'm here to help sick people."

Kevorkian, 61, is a retired pathologist. He has seen enough death to decide that sometimes it's a good idea.

That line of thought makes him unpopular in the closed and cautious world of medicine. To those he cannot offend with talk of euthanasia, he also delivers stinging discourses on the "dark-age hypocrites" in medicine, religion and politics.

"People tell me, 'Use a little more tact. Don't be so strident,' " he says. "But that's not fun. If I'm going to be ignored, I want to enjoy it a little bit."

He is resigned to being a buzzing gadfly. Thin, ascetic, with an oversized nose and white, swept-back hair, he looks like an Armenian Leprechaun. His button-down sweater and double-knit slacks are green. His brown eyes are bright and his suede desert boots are so worn they're shiny.

"I could have been rich," he says. "I could have been a professor if I wanted to play by their rules. There's nothing wrong with that if you want a yacht, but I don't want a yacht."

Kevorkian lives in a one-bedroom apartment above a shop in downtown Royal Oak, drives a rusty 1968 Volkswagen van and subsists largely on cheese sandwiches. He spends his days in libraries, researching articles on euthanasia for whatever foreign or fringe journals will publish them. At night, he reads — nonfiction only, "something I'm going to learn from" — and tinkers with his machine.

"I want to make euthanasia a positive thing," he says. What good is anguish? Why stay in the ring when you no longer want to fight? Kevorkian puts the questions to thin air, then answers them with a zealot's passion.

"Religious dogma has become part of the marrow of humanity. We can't get rid of it. There should be absolutely no connection between medicine and religion, but there is, and it's paralyzing."

His research tells him that the Greeks practiced euthanasia in the time of Hippocrates. He says condemned criminals in ancient Egypt were sometimes killed in the lab, giving their all to science. Now that we can transplant pieces from one body to the next, he wonders, why do we waste so many of them?

He wants death row inmates to be able to offer their bodies for harvest. Put them to sleep, pluck their organs and save several lives even as one is ended. "Every execution you read about in the paper," he says, "means the death of six to eight people."

He started corresponding with convicts during his residency at the University of Michigan in the 1950s. That began an absorption with euthanasia that finally led, last October, to the construction of the prototype mercy killer.

Today's streamlined model, the third, stands 20 inches high and measures 14 inches across. It's a simple frame holding three glass bottles — one of saline solution, to keep the intravenous line open; one of pentathol, to induce coma, and one of potassium chloride to stop the heart.

The plan calls for Kevorkian to insert the IV. Then it will be up to the patient to press a button, start the flow of pentathol and die.

Some experts say Kevorkian could be guilty of homicide for providing the means of death. Others say he is not liable, because he would not actually administer the drugs.

Kevorkian expects to be prosecuted. "Philosophical cowards," he snorts. He doesn't care. He believes in the machine.

He may even use it himself someday.

"I don't want to suffer when I die," he says. "Do unto others what you will do for yourself."

The Golden Rule. It's religion, but he can live with it.

— *Neal Rubin*

FREE PRESS FILE PHOTO

THE SINGULAR DOCTOR

This article appeared in the Free Press on Feb. 3, 1991, about midway between Jack Kevorkian's first and next assisted suicide.

Dr. Death is all wound up — his eyes alight and his voice animated, shouting one minute, whispering the next — as he recalls his wicked triumph during an oil painting course he took almost 30 years ago.

It was a night course, at a junior high school in Pontiac. The crusading young pathologist found himself in a classroom with mostly little old ladies of decidedly conventional taste.

"I look around," Jack Kevorkian recalls, "and everyone is painting clowns and trees and little kitties, and ... UGH!"

Kevorkian says "Ugh" as if he's just encountered a murdered clown or a drowned kitty. He grimaces. He puts his hands up as if to push the images away. "I just do NOT like anything banal, you know what I mean?"

"I says: I'll show them. I'll paint something that will turn their stomachs, and then I'll quit this course. I was going to quit anyway, so I'll paint something that they'll get sick looking at, and I'll just leave."

His first painting, as described by the artist:

"It was a skull, with the top of the skull leaning back a little, the jaw twisted to one side, like it's kind of laughing out of the side of its face. It had a couple of teeth missing, a couple of gold teeth, and it's on red velvet, folded so it looks almost like a tongue inside of it.

"Then, there were some bones coming underneath, and a broken femur under the thing, and then out of the eye socket is coming an iris — a flower — and the iris has got a little aura around it, and merges with darker blue and black in the background.

"Tacked up on the wall behind, where you can hardly see it, I have this pasty yellow-green skin, peeled off the head and hanging there."

"I called it 'Very Still Life.' "

"And people were looking at it," he says, beaming, his voice ringing with pride, "and it was a sensation! The exact reverse of what I thought!"

He savors that moment, this 62-year-old guy who is taking so much flak now. Sure, a few people were put off by that painting, but it grabbed them. It provoked the attention of anybody who glanced its way. It was exhibited at a string of colleges, along with other equally quirky Kevorkian paintings entitled "Fever" and "Nausea" and "Coma."

"Nobody could pass by without noticing, and reacting," he says. "That's what it's all about, right?"

The paintings are lost, part of a waylaid shipment of possessions Kevorkian had stored in California. He is also bereft of his furniture, his organ, his harpsichord, books, pictures, many of his personal records — everything, really, of any value.

"It's awful," he says, and suggests he knows something of his Armenian parents' feelings when they lost everything under siege by the Turks.

On the other hand, it is liberating. "I have nothing to lose," he often remarks these days when explaining why it is he who is at the center of the firestorm over physician-assisted suicide. "Other doctors can't do what I do, because they have responsibilities to people I don't have, and they have families, and positions to protect."

Jack Kevorkian is unemployed. He is unmarried. He has scant possessions, few friends. He can take any risk and cross any line and break any taboo, including the Big One — the one that has fascinated him all his life, the one about which he painted his first alarming artwork: Death.

So he crossed the line. Became famous, and probably became permanently unemployable as well. Maybe he already was. William Beaumont Hospital in Oakland County turned him down for a lowly paramedic's job two years ago, and Kevorkian knew then he was a pariah. Still, he went on writing his crusading articles about euthanasia; he kept up his research; he built his little $30 machine.

He insists it's the issue of assisted suicide that needed to become famous, not Dr. Jack Kevorkian.

"I agree to help you ... in the spirit of rationality, which you are about to lose," Kevorkian told 54-year-old Alzheimer's patient Janet Adkins in a conversation two days before her death, videotaped and shown at the hearing when he was charged with her murder.

He couldn't find an apartment, a hotel, a nursing home or ambulance to accommodate them. So he answered the pleadings of Adkins and her husband by offering his white 1968 Volkswagen van. He drove to a public park. He punctured her arm four times before getting the needle in firmly, and she pushed the button on his suicide device — releasing a tranquilizer, then poison into her veins.

"The highest ethical principle to me is individual self-determination," Kevorkian intones on the videotape. It's not that hard to believe. It's more difficult to believe he didn't anticipate the explosion Adkins' appointment with Dr. Death — as he doesn't mind having been dubbed — would set off.

And it's near impossible to think he's not getting a kick out of all the attention now.

"People are looking at this out there," Kevorkian says to Adkins on the tape, sounding like the talk-show hosts who would later beat a path to his door. "Some say you're doing the wrong thing. What would you tell them?"

Adkins, an apple-cheeked woman in a red blouse with a bow, doesn't rise to the call to speechify. "That I just ... I want out," she replies firmly, but with no verbal flourish.

She got out June 4, 1990. The end was quiet and unobserved except by the doctor she'd come from Oregon to see, and one of the doctor's sisters, who thinks him a genius. "Yea, though, I walk through the valley of the shadow of death, I will fear no evil: for thou art with me," the sister read from the 23rd Psalm as Adkins looked up at her deliverer.

Potassium chloride stopped her heart, and Jack Kevorkian caused a sensation again.

"You know, they skipped me up a grade in sixth because I caused a teacher to cry."

Kevorkian is talking about his school days in Pontiac. He was often bored, he says, and even then, it was unbearable.

"I was throwing paper wads," he says, demonstrating with a flicked wrist and making one of those explosion sounds little boys make, "and shooting at the clock. I was bothering others, see, and she couldn't control me."

The teacher put her head down on the desk and began to sob. Then, she went downstairs to see the principal, and Jack got the summons.

"I was really afraid," he says, intently, half a century later. "The principal was a formidable figure, no sense of humor at all. She wore these — what do you call them? — pince-nez glasses."

Jack went in to face the music, and the principal told him to pack up his books and report to the junior high school the next day. Almost immediately, Kevorkian was happier; the lessons were more of a challenge.

He says he still feels badly about upsetting the young female teacher. But he's also clearly proud, telling a tale about how he was something special.

This is a lesson Jack Kevorkian seems to have learned early: Struggle to be mentally stimulated. Cause a commotion if you must. You might get in trouble, but it's worth it.

He still insists, no matter what, on following his exceedingly active mind wherever it takes him.

Kevorkian lives abstemiously. He wakes in his dark, dumpy little apartment on Main Street in Royal Oak, where he sleeps on a single bed mattress on the floor. He has dry toast, with perhaps a little jelly for breakfast — a can of corn and a pear for lunch.

He sits in the tiny, windowless living room, at a desk made from plywood, graced by cardboard file boxes scavenged from the alley, and answers correspondence about euthanasia from people from all over the world.

He hops on an old bicycle of his sister's — even in winter — and rides to medical seminars at Beaumont Hospital, several miles away; his old VW van was impounded by the police.

He practices his flute or reads, and in the evenings maybe watches a little TV. Movies are rare; about 20 years ago, he went to see "M*A*S*H," and the language was so vile, the violence so explicit, that he walked out.

Partly, this spare lifestyle is due to lack of funds. Kevorkian lives on Social Security, since he became eligible on his birthday in May, plus a little savings from before he left his last job eight years ago.

But partly, it's personal choice. Dr. Herbert Swanson, a friend from Kevorkian's days as a resident at Detroit Receiving Hospital, recalls how delighted Kevorkian was at the debut of the Ford Escort: "It was so stripped down and free of frills — the perfect economy car."

Frills don't thrill him. It is ideas that go off like firecrackers, and thoughts that alarm, that provide all the excitement in Kevorkian's life.

"I can't understand why they're so afraid of the truth!" he rails when a medical journal turns down a piece on planned death, or medical officials assail his lethal aid to Janet Adkins. "Everybody is afraid to even talk about these things! I am NOT AFRAID."

He doesn't mull why that is. He doesn't really know. His immigrant parents, a housewife and a small-time excavating contractor, were very conventional thinkers, he says — supportive of him, but puzzled about why he had to crusade for such strange things as cadaver transfusions and organ donations by executed criminals when he had made it to respectability as a doctor.

"I just had to, because it was right, and it was honest," he says. "Going through medical school, I knew abortion wasn't immoral and shouldn't be illegal, and I knew euthanasia wasn't immoral, because my mind just wasn't encumbered with all this crap, you know?"

A few people are beginning to appreciate that quality. NBC commentator John Chancellor said in a recent commentary that it is time for new thinking about the ethics of death, and at least Kevorkian has provoked that around the country.

Yet Kevorkian thinks his reasoning should overwhelm. The debate should be over, he declares indignantly; it's obviously a technical knockout. His idea of planned deaths — doesn't everyone see it makes sense?

Kevorkian envisions clinics called "obitoriums" where terminally ill people could make an appointment to die without pain. Arrangements could be made to donate organs, thereby benefiting the living.

"People with Lou Gehrig's disease, with multiple sclerosis, where the brain and nervous system are gone, they're going to die anyway," he says. "They ought to go for what I'm shooting for. What makes it so controversial?"

He throws the question like a gauntlet, daring anyone to come up with a logical argument to combat him. He loves to tear into an issue, take a bite out of his opponent's most cherished belief if he can, and wave the bloody fragment — like a naughty puppy trying to get someone to chase.

And he never gives up. He'll push his views to the fringe, and say things that are beyond what he really does mean, while he's hyped up on the stimulant of having his say.

"The pope runs the state, not (Gov. John) Engler," he snaps. He calls the legal system that's come after him "a resurgence of the Inquisition."

Railing about the torment of the Armenian people, he is disdainful of the Jewish Holocaust: "I wish my forefathers went through what the Jews did," he scoffs. "The Jews were gassed. Armenians were killed in every conceivable way. Pregnant women were split open with bayonets and babies taken out. They were drowned, burned, heads were smashed in vices. They were chopped in half.

"So, the Holocaust doesn't interest me, see? They've had a lot of publicity, but they didn't suffer as much."

He may not be capable of subtlety.

He is capable of lighter thoughts — and wit. Even whimsy.

"A baker from old Dusseldorf," begins the limerick he wrote on a summer's eve, while sitting on Main Street outside his apartment with the younger man who lives across the hall. Somehow, the name Dusseldorf came up, and 'twixt the two of them, they twisted a twist.

A baker from old Dusseldorf
Used to hawk his wares on the wharf.
When business got slow,
'cause he ran out of dough,
He'd buy shortening bread from a dwarf.

"OK, if you don't like it, you've got to vomit right now!" he insists. Honesty. He won't have it any other way.

There are a lot of things he won't have any other way but his. He decided not to marry a young store clerk 22 years ago because he decided she wasn't self-disciplined enough. And she had a promiscuous sister. He didn't want to put up with that.

"I can see," says his old high school chum Suzanne Robinson, who also never married, "how he would be a difficult man to live with. So certain of everything."

And yet, sometimes, so boyish and blithe. He chortles about the time he put Polish sausage under the microscope at the pathology lab so everybody could see exactly what they were eating. He loves television cartoons, especially Sylvester the Cat. He is a devotee of astrology — just as a pretext, he says, to talk about personality — but he knows all the signs of the zodiac, and he has an opinion on each prognosticator. (Sydney Omarr is legit, but Jeanne Dixon is an absolute fraud.)

He is funny, if you appreciate irreverence and teasing. Even if you don't, he'll try to twit you.

Last spring, when he went to a suburban newspaper office to get a little publicity for his new machine with its three hanging bottles and lethal button, he walked in on a chilly day, offered his unmittened hand, and chirped: "Cold as a cadaver, eh?"

The reporter's jaw dropped.

"My humor offends people, sometimes," he says, "because I use them as foils to amuse myself." Kevorkian shrugs. "Geminis are like that."

He can make the joke at his own expense, though. He is in mid-rant about how the medical profession would like to burn him at the stake when someone joshes that a picture of that would win the Pulitzer Prize. "Nah." he says, tickled. "I'd look awful when the clothes burn off.

"I got bow legs."

In fact, he seems to see himself pretty clearly, even when taking a cold, hard look. Here is Jack Kevorkian, listing his faults:

"I'm hypercritical.

"I lose my temper, and feel terrible afterward. I say to myself, I shouldn't have done that! Shouldn't have said that! Should have kept quiet.

"I'm cynical, but not cynical enough, because insincerity really gets to me, you know?"

His biggest mistake, he admits, was in not marrying: "That's shirking responsibility as a human being. From nature's standpoint, I'm immoral." He couldn't steel himself to the possibility of a breakup. If he didn't find a perfectly compatible mate — one whose goals, skills, and station in life were complementary to his — then it wasn't worth trying, he figured.

"So, now there's no one alive with my name," he says wistfully. "My male relatives were killed in Armenia, and I never built a family."

He has remained a solitary figure during the huge publicity storm. The sister who read the psalm in the van, Flora Holzheimer, went back to Germany, where she lives with her family.

The other one, Margo Janus of Troy, who sat outside the van in her Plymouth Reliant keeping watch that day, did come to court during his trial for Adkins' death. "Liar, liar!" she hissed at the prosecutor one day. After that, she decided it was better to stay home. A few acquaintances from long ago, such as Suzanne Robinson, also showed up to lend support.

"But really it's me, alone," Kevorkian says. "That doesn't bother me. I've gotten used to that."

He was always something of a loner. Now, he is something of a leper.

"I never really fit in," Kevorkian muses, "but I did used to feel at least that I belonged to a healing profession. They don't think so any more — and I don't, either."

Kevorkian can't think of any medical heroes, except maybe Dr. Albert Schweitzer, and that's really because he was an organist and a Bach lover like Kevorkian. He admires Nelson Mandela and Libyan leader Moammar Qaddafi — "he's blunt! he's honest!" — but there aren't any true leaders like that in medicine, he says.

It seems he was destined for disappointment and isolation. The medical world isn't a place for intellectual rabble-rousers. He got the word about that early on.

He was in his second year of residency at the University of Michigan medical school in Ann Arbor in 1957 when he was assigned to research the history of the autopsy. The aspiring pathologist was excited about the task. Most of the old articles were written in German, and he knew the language. He had begun studying it — and also Japanese — at Pontiac High School when the country was embroiled in World War II.

Kevorkian got even more excited when he found an old article about the ancient Ptolemies, who decreed that condemned prisoners must be executed in medical laboratories. The Ptolemies' thinking was that criminals owed society a debt, and they could pay in part by giving their bodies for research.

"I figured, I'll introduce the requirement that the condemned man consent, and that anesthesia be used for the execution, and that idea can fly today!"

He went and visited a prison in Ohio and talked to men on death row; they liked the idea. He wrote up an article and sent it out for publication.

"Oh, brother," Kevorkian groans. "I was naive as hell."

No publication would take the article. After a while, he did manage to get permission to speak about it at a medical seminar in Washington, D.C. — and made national headlines, which embarrassed U-M. The late Dr. Adam French, then chairman of the pathology department and a man Kevorkian esteemed, called him in and told him flatly: Drop this condemned criminal stuff, or leave the university.

"It bothered me, but not that much," says Kevorkian. There was a doctor shortage in those days, and he knew he could get another job.

He went to Pontiac General Hospital in his old hometown and continued his residency, then took a year off to do research in Europe, and returned to work at the old Receiving Hospital in Detroit. By then, Kevorkian had another hot research idea.

He'd read about a method of determining the moment of death, developed in the mid-19th Century, by looking into the eye with an opthalmoscope.

"I asked them to let me work on it at night. I made what I called Death Rounds. I used to joke about it. Once I made a black arm band and started walking around looking for anybody dying in the hospital."

That's when people began calling him Dr. Death. Other hospital employees would watch him peering into the eyes of a patient who'd just passed away, and ask, "Why? What value does this have?"

Kevorkian would tell them: It is important to know the point past which a person cannot be revived. Later, when organ transplants were pioneered in the early '60s, he'd point to that as a good reason to pinpoint death.

"But really, my number one reason was because it was interesting," he says, "and my second reason was because it was a taboo subject."

Back at Pontiac Hospital where he returned in 1959, a colleague told him about a new report on some innovative work by Russian doctors. They were taking blood from cadavers and transfusing it to humans. Again, he was fascinated. And as a staff pathologist, running the hospital blood bank was one of his duties; this was right up his alley!

He got a crew of staff members fired up about helping with the research, and he still talks of their wild experiments as "the best days of our lives."

"It had to be a sudden death, see. We had to do an autopsy real quick. Then we took the blood out of the jugular vein. I devised my own system where we'd tilt the table with the body up, put the needle in the jugular, and the blood would run down to a vacuum bottle.

"We gave the blood to an old lady, terminally ill, whose family said OK — and everything worked just fine."

Then it occurred to him that one place where the transfusion technique would be helpful was on the battlefield, where often a freshly dead soldier would be lying right next to a wounded man in dire need of blood. A direct transfusion! Blood flowing out of the corpse, and into the live body.

Several technicians stepped forward to volunteer as the live guinea pigs to attempt such a transfusion.

One night, a corpse arrived — a 14-year-old girl, the victim of a car crash, and DOA in the emergency room. She had the same blood type as one of the volunteers, a 35-year-old woman who was on duty that night. Kevorkian had the volunteer lie down on the table, connecting her via tubing and syringe to the dead teen.

Everyone was excited and nervous. This was virgin ground. Not even the Russians had done this.

Kevorkian went for the teenager's jugular — but he couldn't find it. As with Janet Adkins 30 years later, the vein eluded him. He found out later the girl's neck was broken and the vein distended. But right then, he had to think fast.

"So I says, OK, and I just plunge the needle into her heart. I drew the blood slowly and then I put it slowly into the technician, with the syringe."

Kevorkian asked the tech how she felt, and she said OK, but there was a funny taste in her mouth. His knees almost buckled with fear. "What am I doing?" he thought. "Poisoning her?"

The next day the results of the tests on the dead girl showed a blood alcohol content of 0.35. She was surpassingly drunk. Could the tech have been tasting liquor? Other doctors are skeptical; Kevorkian believes it.

Kevorkian wrote up his research. He made national headlines again, even more and bigger this time, including a spread in Time magazine. He applied for a grant to continue the research. He got turned down.

"First the university telling me to leave. Now this. That's why I'm hard on medicine: The establishment is extremely corrupt."

In the late '70s, after a couple of decades of work in Michigan, he struck out for California, finding a post at Beverly Hills Medical Center in Los Angeles and living out of the white VW van for a while, because it was so hard to find a cheap apartment.

In 1981, he took a job at Pacific Hospital in Long Beach, which he held for a year, and where his former boss, Dr. Fred Hodell, found his work "brilliant."

The renegade has never been fired. He has bounced around a lot, and sometimes found it hard to get along with superiors. Still, his competence kept his reputation clean.

Over the years, though, his actual work testing tissue and blood became somewhat routine — and therefore less important. His groundbreaking research on death, the issues that brought him notoriety and rejection, never bored him — and became crucial. In 1982, he quit the job at Pacific to concentrate on his research.

He churned out articles on euthanasia, planned death and rational suicide. "Are you serious???" incredulous editors would write across his manuscripts. But some did get published, including "The Last Fearsome Taboo"; "Marketing of Human Organs and Tissues is Justified and Necessary," and "The Long Overdue Medical Specialty: Bioethiatrics."

He kept hammering away at his research-on-condemned-criminals idea, and began attacking the medical establishment that disdained him.

"Physicians tend to be conformists by instinct and training," he wrote in a 1986 article for the journal of Medicine and Law, "and would therefore shun as ostensibly immoral anything not sanctified by prevailing public opinion or pending legislation."

"Hypocrisy! Phoniness to the core," he blusters now, sounding like a senior citizen Holden Caulfield from "Catcher in the Rye." Since the death of Janet Adkins, Kevorkian has been pilloried as never before. His own rhetoric has escalated to new extremes.

Certainly, he has his supporters. Letters to the editor run in his favor nationwide, and opinion polls indicate the majority of the public agrees with him on the issues. Hundreds have written to ask for his help; some simply send money. Autograph seekers approach him in the grocery store. Mary Tyler Moore shook his hand, and told him to keep up the good work, when he saw her on the set of CBS's morning news show.

But other doctors give him a wide berth. They say Kevorkian put a black mark on the profession by acting unethically — and shabbily too, in the back of a van, wearing a golf hat, and hand-printing Adkins' wish to donate her corneas on a piece of notebook paper instead of using hospital forms.

"Veterinary medicine," sniffed Dr. John Finn, medical director of the Hospice of Southeastern Michigan. He called for Kevorkian's license to be revoked.

Others were quietly appalled at the media circus surrounding this doctor who seemed to have an inappropriately messianic gleam in his eye, and got a thrill out of going to jail in a pair of sweatpants with PRISONER in big letters down the leg.

Some doctors are privately for him, Kevorkian is certain. And he believes that quite a few have secretly done the same as he — provided a terminally ill patient with the means to die. But this just makes him angrier.

"What good is it, subterfuge?" he shouts. "How are people going to know which doctor to go to, what's available to them? You've got to be OPEN! You gotta do it right, be honest. If not, nothing will ever change."

He wonders if it will be in his lifetime. Will Jack Kevorkian be a cold cadaver before the dreadfully ill and dying can opt for their own demise, and get help from a compassionate physician?

The Michigan Legislature is headed toward passage of a law to prevent just that. And later this week, Circuit Judge Alice Gilbert will rule on the Oakland County prosecutor's request for a permanent injunction against use of the suicide machine. But Kevorkian says no matter what, he'll spend his remaining years lobbying for the right of planned death.

"In another state maybe," he says. "I could go somewhere else if they pass that law against me here."

He won't use the little machine again in Michigan, though. He says it was only for preliminary research anyway, to show how it could be done, and then doctors were supposed to come together and talk about setting up regulated clinics. He doesn't even have the machine in his possession. The prosecutors took it.

He could build another any time, of course. On the set of CBS, when the producers demanded a model, he threw one together in 10 minutes — from spare items laying around in nearby offices.

Perhaps he'll have to make one for himself someday. Right now, he's extremely fit. He climbs trees and walks fences for fun. In jail, another prisoner, just a sprout, complimented him on his physique. But what if some affliction should strike?

He could insert the needle — he's drawn his own blood before, even surgically removed his own moles. He could press the button.

Is Dr. Death afraid of death?

It has hurt him badly a couple of times. His father died suddenly of heart failure when Kevorkian was 33 — and he experienced a major depression. His mother went slowly, painfully, nine years later. There was cancer all through her bones. She was doped up and incoherent at the end.

He dreams of them sometimes still. He wakes up, and wonders, What was that? What are we? What happens in death, besides the decay of our physical being?

"If you don't have any sort of faith, you think of the big nothingness," he says. "And you wonder what is this brief span of consciousness? What is all this? All thinking people go through this — you just don't talk about it. There's no answer, anyway."

Jack Kevorkian has no living will to specify when life-support should be removed if he should end up in the hospital like his mother. He assumes everyone knows what he wants.

He just hopes he can go out calmly and rationally, the way he believes Adkins did. "She was very calm," Kevorkian says. "She dreaded what would have come. I would too. I don't want to die of Alzheimer's — smeared with your own urine and feces, don't know who you are. Come on!"

In the courtroom during Kevorkian's hearing, the disposition of Janet Adkins' body parts were discussed in great detail. Pathologists and medical examiners told how they harvested her blood, urine, liver, kidney, muscle and spleen; how they smeared them on slides and packaged them in baggies, and shipped them UPS to other labs.

It was gory stuff, unsettling at the least. But it didn't bother Kevorkian one bit. He is quite sure his patient rests in peace.

— Antoinette Martin

THE KEVORKIAN CREW

JACK KEVORKIAN, 68, is a retired pathologist who worked at hospitals in Detroit, Pontiac, Ann Arbor, Wyandotte and California. No longer has any medical license. Arranges and supervises assisted suicides.

GEOFFREY FIEGER, 46, successful, media-savvy lawyer retained by Kevorkian in 1990, has won three criminal acquittals for him and gained national fame; usually the spokesman after an assisted suicide.

MARGARET (Margo) JANUS, Kevorkian's sister and one of the most dedicated believers in assisted suicide, died in September 1994 at age 68. She was present for more than 15 of his assisted suicides and kept the records of them.

MICHAEL SCHWARTZ, 49, Fieger's law partner, makes frequent appearances on Kevorkian's behalf; nicknamed "the barracuda" when he was chewing up errant lawyers as chief prosecutor for the Michigan Attorney Grievance Commission.

NEAL NICOL, 58,
is a salesman of medical supplies, including carbon monoxide, which has been used in Kevorkian suicides. Nicol's Waterford Township home has been the site of at least five of the deaths.

JANET GOOD, 73,
of Farmington Hills is a Kevorkian ally who frequently accompanies him to assisted suicides and is herself dying of cancer. She faces criminal charges of aiding in an Ionia County death.

GEORGES REDING, 71, of Galesburg is a Belgian-born psychiatrist who has practiced in Michigan since 1990. He has attended at least six Kevorkian-assisted suicides and appeared with Kevorkian at the National Press Club in Washington.

MICHAEL ROWADY, 24,
is a University of Detroit Law School student who works with Fieger. He has frequently appeared to identify the bodies of Kevorkian suicides, carrying the driver's license or other items from the deceased.

JOHN LUKE

FIEGER: BEYOND BLUSTER

This article appeared in the Free Press on Oct. 3, 1996. At this point Jack Kevorkian had assisted in at least 42 suicides.

"In this world, if you do not say a thing in an irritating way, you may just as well not say it at all, because people will not trouble themselves about anything that does not trouble them."
— *George Bernard Shaw,*
a quote written in one of Geoffrey Fieger's law books

Ladies and gentleman of the jury:

This man, Geoffrey Fieger, has been in our faces since 1990, shortly after Dr. Jack Kevorkian's first assisted suicide, the death of Janet Adkins.

As Kevorkian's attorney, Fieger has been in the news, on the news, on the radio, at post-suicide scenes, in court, on TV, on Court TV and, with numbing frequency, in his office giving news conferences.

We have heard him say the f-word, the sh-word, the g-d word, the a-word and the s-o-b word.

No one escapes a Fieger opinion. We have watched him tell Detroit Cardinal Adam Maida to "put up or shut up" on assisted suicide. He has called Gov. John Engler a "fat, ugly sonofabitch" and asked whether Engler's triplets have curly tails. He has told Michigan Court of Appeals judges to stop acting like "squirrels, mollusks and lizards."

Fieger has pinned a clown nose on a blown-up picture of Oakland County Prosecutor Richard Thompson, told religious groups to go to hell, described Jesus Christ as "just some goofball who got nailed to the cross," and told his own famous client, in court, to shut up.

He has tried to drag through public mud Dr. L.J. Dragovic, the Oakland County medical examiner who has had the audacity to declare assisted suicides homicides.

He has alienated or intimidated countless lawyers and more than a few judges.

But, ladies and gentlemen ...

Geoffrey Fieger also has won, by his count, more than $100 million for people in courtroom verdicts and lawsuit settlements. For Kevorkian, he has not only beaten the system, he has made fools of its defenders.

He has defeated his most determined opponent, Thompson, twice in court, and then took credit when Thompson lost his job in a Republican primary.

Fieger, by way of Kevorkian, has become famous. He has been profiled in major U.S. and European publications. He's had national TV crews follow him around, he often appears on TV programs such as "Good Morning America," and at one time cohosted a radio talk show on WJR-AM (760).

If all goes well, 45-year-old Fieger may soon have his own syndicated TV talk show, "Fieger Now," a notion that probably horrifies his critics.

The point, ladies and gentlemen, is this: Geoffrey Fieger will be in our faces for some time to come. And after all the trials, news conferences, insults and attacks, he is no longer just a man or just an attorney. He has become a caricature, so overexposed, obnoxious and offensive, so often the target of potshots, that we cannot trust what we think we know about him.

So, what is Geoffrey Fieger really all about?

Let's examine the evidence.

Once, many years ago, Geoffrey Fieger was just ... Geoff Fieger.

He was a big, aimless, aggressive kid who grew up in a happy, stormy home with a small circle of people who shaped him. He is loyal to all of them — especially his parents.

"The thing that I like most about Geoffrey Fieger — and I do love him," says Janet Good, founder of the Michigan chapter of the Hemlock Society, which advocates assisted suicide, "is how well he speaks of his parents and how well he treats his mother."

But no one affected Fieger more than his father.

Bernard Fieger was a Jewish, Harvard-educated lawyer who joined the civil rights crusade in Mississippi. He opened one of the Detroit area's first interracial law firms. He was talented, articulate, aggressive and explosive. Geoffrey grew up to be just like him, and the two thundered famously at one another when Geoffrey joined his father's firm in 1979. (When Geoffrey signed on, the other partners quit.)

But beneath the thunder was Geoffrey's thirst for his father's approval. Fieger says today his father did show approval in his own way. Others aren't so sure.

"Some people think Geoffrey's an ogre in the office. His dad was worse," says Keenie Fieger, Geoffrey's wife. "The walls used to shake. He was really gruff. And Geoffrey was saying 'Look Dad, I won, whatever it was, a million,' and his dad would say, 'So what are you going to do tomorrow?' And then it was, Oh, I've got to do better, I've got to do better."

Fieger was deeply affected by his father's death in 1988. Bernard's long suffering from complications of diabetes probably figured into his son's ready acceptance later of Kevorkian's assisted-suicide crusade.

Fieger has never removed his father's name from the door of his Southfield law firm, Fieger, Fieger & Schwartz.

Fieger's mother, June, is Norwegian by descent and a teacher by profession who also worked as a union organizer. She kept a picket sign in her trunk and loved nothing better than rabble-rousing on picket lines. June Fieger also taught one of the Detroit area's first sex education classes.

Now semiretired, she lives in a West Bloomfield Township home that Geoffrey bought, gutted and refurbished for her.

"I've always gone by the saying, 'Don't judge me by my friends, they may like me for many reasons. Judge me by my enemies, for I choose them very carefully,' " she says.

Her son, the oldest of her three children, seems to have taken that to heart, except he isn't too fussy about enemies.

Fieger's brother, Doug, gained fame with the rock band the Knack, known for the hit, "My Sharona." Doug lives in California, as does Fieger's sister, Beth Fieger Falkenstein, a TV scriptwriter. Both declined to comment for this article.

When they were under the same roof, family members apparently communicated best through confrontation. Detente was not an issue.

"I thought, this is wild," Keenie Fieger recalls of her first meetings with the Fiegers. "I've never seen anything like it."

Tall and forceful, Geoffrey could be a bully to his little brother, June Fieger recalls, and he spoke his mind. Always early-to-bed, early-to-rise, he went to sleep with the sun "and he'd tell everybody to shut up," his mother says, chuckling.

A few other people also touched Fieger's life. He admires his uncle, Walter Eugene Oberer, dean of the University of Utah's law school, and his Norwegian grandmother, who helped raise Geoffrey and kept her house spotless. She may have influenced's Geoffrey's compulsive neatness. He called her Ma; June he called Mother.

And there was Jimmy Jefferson, the Fieger firm's janitor for many years. Fieger says Jefferson was uneducated but "very wise," and Fieger loved him. When Jefferson developed cancer, Fieger sued his doctors for diagnosing Jefferson too late, and won a settlement of about $50,000.

For the duration of Jefferson's illness, "Geoffrey stopped by to bring him lunch and milk shakes," June Fieger recalls. "He went to make sure he ate. He shaved him regularly, for as long as Jimmy was sick. He's not, like, 'Hire somebody else to do that.' He did it."

Fieger paid for Jefferson's funeral, gave an impassioned eulogy and then took everyone to dinner. Today, a plaque designates the law library at Fieger's firm as the W.J. Jefferson Library.

Fieger attended Oak Park public schools. He was a decent student who loved theater and sports. He was a lineman in football, wrestled and swam. He dated one girl at a time, usually a blond, and drove a Volkswagen Beetle.

As a teenager, Fieger was nearly killed in the Bug when he was rammed at an intersection. His mother bought him a sturdy Volvo. He still has it, and has driven Volvos ever since. Michigan's most flamboyant lawyer says he likes Volvos because they are staid and safe.

Fieger graduated from Oak Park High School in 1969. In 1974 and 1976, he earned his bachelor's degree in theater and master's degree in speech from the University of Michigan. For a while, he hung out in Europe, then decided to pursue a doctorate.

June Fieger remembers telling her son, "You can get your PhD in sand tile if you want, but I'm not paying for it." She suggested law school.

Fieger figured what the hell. He entered Detroit College of Law and fell in love with the world of judges, juries and verbal combat.

About the same time, Fieger also fell in love with Kathleen (Keenie) Podwoiski, a reserved, attractive woman from Garden City. She had been a bridesmaid in a mutual friend's wedding. They attended Shakespeare plays, jogged, worked out and listened to each other's music: hers, jazz and classical; his, rock and roll ("Who's the Knack?" she asked him).

"I thought he was quite unusual myself," Keenie recalls. "I had never seen anyone so self-confident." He was intelligent, funny, asked "a billion" questions about her, and then talked a lot about himself.

They were married in 1983, seven years before a phone call from a retired pathologist put Geoffrey Fieger onto center stage of public opinion.

In August 1990, 62-year-old Jack Kevorkian stood in Oakland County Circuit Court, representing himself in a legal battle with Thompson, who was seeking a court order to stop Kevorkian from assisting in more suicides.

Friends — and the judge — told Kevorkian to get a lawyer.

So on a Sunday, he called the offices of Fieger, Fieger & Schwartz.

"Jack doesn't realize that most people don't work on Sundays," Fieger says, laughing.

But on this hot Sunday, Fieger happened to be in. He had stopped by his office to cool off after attending a polo match with Keenie.

Kevorkian had seen Fieger on TV, supervising the removal of furniture from William Beaumont Hospital in Royal Oak because the hospital had balked at paying a malpractice judgment won by Fieger.

Kevorkian liked that.

Fieger immediately invited Kevorkian and his sister, Margo Janus, to come by the office. The two men were — and still are — cosmic opposites.

Kevorkian, a small man built like a well-fed scarecrow, has short white hair and dark, sharp eyes. A lifelong bachelor, he lived at the time in a small, windowless and sparsely furnished apartment in Royal Oak.

"He was practicing for solitary confinement," Fieger jokes.

An odd but sincere man, Kevorkian shops at the Salvation Army and eats like a refugee. He was born in 1928 in Pontiac after his parents immigrated to the United States to escape Turkey's extermination of the Armenians.

Kevorkian is a 1952 graduate of the University of Michigan School of Medicine and a well-read, learned man who loves philosophy, history and art. He is an atheist and is afraid to fly. He isn't crazy about fame, but lets Fieger drag him to public appearances. He has resisted movie and book deals and the lecture circuit, where, Fieger says, he could make a fortune.

Kevorkian does not smoke or drink alcohol and rarely curses. He is a loner by nature, a man with an interest in death that many consider macabre.

And, when he met Fieger, Kevorkian considered himself a failure. His ideas for death-related experiments had crippled his career as a pathologist; assisted suicide was not a public issue; he was alone and regretted never marrying.

Fieger, 39 at the time, was already a successful trial lawyer specializing in personal injury and medical malpractice cases. His resume boasted of winning in 1982, just three years out of law school, the first million-dollar judgment in the United States based on misuse of antipsychotic drugs.

At 6-feet-2 and 225 pounds, Fieger fusses over his appearance and favors blue pin-striped suits. He reads mostly magazines and newspapers, flies all over the world, covets publicity, cusses by second nature and loves vodka. He will be dead before he ever considers himself a failure.

Kevorkian recalls that after they met, he was not inclined to hire Fieger.

"I wasn't ready to pick anyone then, really," Kevorkian says. "I was being forced into it and I was still reluctant. My sister talked me into it."

But, Kevorkian says, "I got the idea early on that he felt deep down that this is the right kind of issue. I don't know if he was convinced or not, but I felt he felt it was right. And … he believed in it enough to help me for my benefit."

Some in the legal community considered Fieger an unlikely choice to defend Kevorkian. His track record was in civil, not criminal, law. Given events of the past six years, it seems fair to say they were wrong, although many still refuse to concede that, Fieger says.

"The implication is that I win in spite of myself," he says.

Fieger has never been a shrinking violet. Long before Kevorkian, he was a pit bull, as evidenced by the furniture-moving scene at Beaumont. Fieger also spent years fighting a drunken-driving charge in Washtenaw County, costing taxpayers thousands of dollars as he appealed all the way to the Michigan Supreme Court.

Fieger argued he was innocent. But the verdict stood.

Kevorkian has put Fieger's less likable characteristics into near constant practice. He has earned more enemies than his mother ever dreamed of. And he has made himself a target.

But if it bothers him, it rarely shows. He never backs down or apologizes. He approaches adversaries like opposing linemen in football games — head-on.

Allow me to disparage you mildly, reads a sign on his office door, for soon I shall excoriate the entire family of your enemies.

For the record, critics say Fieger has a habit of stretching the truth beyond recognition, or he just tells outright lies, then backtracks with great bluster.

"More than once, he will lie," says Michael Modelski, former Oakland County assistant prosecutor who handled the injunction against Kevorkian before going into private practice. "In fact, once he got into the case, an attorney called me and said, 'Let me warn you, if you deal with Fieger, you should have two other people with you: One with a big stick to beat him off you, and another person to just take down whatever he says.'

"He will reverse himself every five minutes. In fact, sometimes he'll lie just to lie, even though the truth may help him more, just to have the power of selling you a lie. It's a game. He'll say things he knows are quotable quotes, that will make a headline, whether they're true or not. He did that all the time.

"If people weren't so afraid of Fieger," Modelski says, "they'd dance on his head."

Fieger's attacks can get so personal and vulgar, they suggest an adolescent who has never learned restraint. During a recent malpractice trial, Fieger denounced his prey, a hospital, in a court hallway, using a locker-room-loud voice.

"I wouldn't send my dog to that place!" he said.

Such behavior is typical, says Yale Kamisar, a criminal law professor at the University of Michigan who opposes assisted suicide.

"He never seems to be willing to admit that anybody who disagrees with him is acting in good faith — they're in the pope's pocket, they're sadists, or they're just plain stupid. He'll caricature someone," he says.

Thomas Kienbaum, president of the State Bar of Michigan, took the unusual step of publicly criticizing Fieger for his outrageous behavior in a letter to the editor of the Detroit News. "I felt I had to do it for my profession," Kienbaum says. "Even plaintiffs' lawyers who are his colleagues come up to me and say, 'I wish you could control the guy.' "

Fieger calls Kienbaum "an ass-licking brownnose" and insists his in-court behavior is fine.

But Fieger is facing disciplinary proceedings before the Attorney Grievance Commission for professional misconduct for his "squirrels, mollusks and lizards" comment and for accusing a prosecutor of covering up a murder.

Fieger says he was simply exercising free speech.

Fieger's friends have told him that his mouth gets him into trouble. He either doesn't listen or can't help himself. Look past all that, most agree, and he's a first-rate lawyer who gives his all for his clients.

With his size, long hair and bronzed face, Fieger has undeniable presence in or out of a courtroom. He seldom walks into court unprepared. And, "his ego does not get in the way of his getting help," said attorney Mayer Morganroth, who assisted Fieger in the last Kevorkian trial.

"The way Geoff is able to absorb facts and then to put them into use — very few can match the way he's able to do that," says Louis Genevie, social psychologist and president of Litigation Strategies in New York, a jury consulting firm Fieger hired for the Kevorkian trials. "He's an incredibly effective communicator. He's been able to take information and spin it into a story."

"I like him," says Oakland County Circuit Judge David Breck, who presided at Kevorkian's third and most recent trial last spring. "I find he can be charming. He's a brilliant guy. But sometimes he's his own worst enemy. He's a zealot."

It was Fieger's well-known ability to sweet-talk juries that probably won the Kevorkian trials. Using essentially the same closing argument for each trial, with variations and without notes, Fieger played on emotion and common sense. He told the juries they could make history.

They did.

"It was the best closing argument I've ever seen," Breck says.

Even Modelski agrees.

"He uses emotion, silence. He uses these nice big displays. He'll blow up pictures of the victims. He'll say, 'You want to see the law in Michigan on assisted suicide? Here it is.' And he puts up this thing, and it's totally blank — 'There is no law!' And things like that. As a showman, he's fantastic. His cross-examinations are usually good, too."

During the Kevorkian injunction hearing, Modelski put a medical ethics expert on the stand.

"I gave Fieger a copy of his resume. It was like 40 pages. And Fieger starts off saying, 'Are you a Nazi?' 'What?!' 'Are you a Nazi? Are you a homosexual?' He threw all this stuff out ... to disconcert (the witness). If you react, you've lost control," Modelski says.

It is widely assumed that Fieger taps his theater training for his arguments to a jury and for his press events.

Rubbish, he says. His abilities as a performer and public speaker predated his theater training. "The first time you try to act in front of the jury or play a role, they will beat the shit out of you. You better be yourself."

And, he says calmly, he is the best.

"There is a certain point that Muhammad Ali realized he was the greatest fighter on earth. I'm positive Wayne Gretzky realized he was the greatest hockey player. And there was a point at which I realized I was as good as they make them," he says.

"I know that sounds conceited, but I just know that I am. I've done everything. I've done civil, I've done criminal, I've done the biggest profile cases. One unique thing that no one ever points out is: Darrow lost Scopes. The Chicago Seven got convicted. Martin Luther King got convicted.

"Kevorkian didn't get convicted. Nobody ever points that out. I mean, not to say they weren't great lawyers. I'm even better, though.

"I understand that the courtroom is a very limited arena. Look at the impressionists — Monet, Picasso — look at Vincent van Gogh. It's not that he didn't know how to paint a picture to look like a photograph. He had gone so far beyond just the basic fundamentals, he could create masterpieces.

"I have such a fundamental understanding of the law. I am able to create things. Every case, I get to paint a new picture, I get to paint a new reality. And that's what makes it fun for me. When I go in there, I create. I'm a master. I'm orchestrating."

Such remarks testify to Fieger's infamous ego — "bigger than all outdoors," says friend and fellow attorney Sheldon Miller. His ego makes Fieger insufferable to many.

But friends and family insist Fieger can be warm, charming and witty. He loves animals and treats his three cats as his children; he knows their birth dates.

He shuns such elite places as country clubs and embraces populist causes. He is loyal to the Detroit area, and can be generous. When he expanded his law firm to an adjoining lot, he donated to charity a home that had to be removed.

In restaurants, "he's very generous at picking up the tab," says the Hemlock Society's Janet Good.

When Good's daughter died unexpectedly last year from a heart attack, "Geoffrey was there all the time. He came to the house, he came to the funeral home.

"He's very overwhelming," Good admits. "He can wilt some people. Some of my friends say, 'How can you stand to be around him?' But if you know him ... he's a teddy bear."

With Fieger, Good says, you must understand: "The play is the thing. Geoffrey is always aware that the play is the thing. When he's in the courtroom, he's focused on that. When he's in a restaurant, he's always aware."

By most accounts, Fieger cares about Kevorkian and about the issue of assisted suicide. And given the nature of these two difficult men, it is fair to suggest that no other lawyer or client could have stood either one of them this long.

The two are like an old married couple. Kevorkian corrects Fieger's English and says he swears too much. Fieger rolls his eyes. They argue in private. They argue in public. They argue in court.

"He's my worst enemy," Fieger says.

Sharing time with them is like dining with the Bickersons. In late summer, after a media interview, the men strode into the hotel bar. Fieger, in a pinstriped three-piece suit, ordered pricey Absolut vodka. Kevorkian, wearing a jersey top, pants, dark green socks and canvas shoes, ordered his usual — a ginger ale with no ice.

"Ice just anesthetizes the taste buds," he said.

Kevorkian remembers the time he fired Fieger.

"He's fired me about 30 million times," Fieger says.

They discuss the house Fieger is renting to Kevorkian for $350 a month. He could get more than $1,000. (Fieger owns five houses, four in Michigan and one in the Caribbean.) It is a very nice house — with windows — on a lake.

"He complains about it every single day," Fieger says.

"I don't like livin' on a lake," Kevorkian says. But he's resigned to staying there, "until the legal things are over. I'm 68. I'll die soon."

Fieger chortles. "He consumes no fat."

They talk nearly every day, " 'Cause I'm his friend," Fieger says. "I worry about him."

When asked if they love each other, Kevorkian grimaces. "Love, schmove! We're friends!"

"Close friends. He doesn't like to express emotion, but I love the guy," Fieger says.

"Aw, listen to 'im!"

Keenie Fieger says her husband thrives on the attention Kevorkian has brought. If a day goes by without it, "I know it's temporary," she says. "It's 'Don't kid yourself, Keenie.' "

Actually, Fieger has a complex, almost incestuous relationship with local reporters. He knows most of them by name. They troop regularly for news conferences to his office, which they call the Fiegerdome. They watch his show, write their stories. And then they interview Fieger ad nauseum whenever they need good copy or sound bites.

But when the scrutiny turns on Fieger, he complains. He was unhappy with reports that Judith Curren, a Boston area woman who killed herself with Kevorkian's help, allegedly had been a victim of domestic violence.

He was also unhappy when newspapers reported that Keenie has twice filed for divorce, and that she has claimed Fieger assaulted her. Fieger says the abuse charge was the product of Keenie's lawyer's overactive imagination.

Keenie declined comment. The divorce file remains active. Fieger says they are working things out. They have no children.

Meanwhile, the Kevorkian cases and news conferences roll on, and no matter what happens, Fieger does, too. Some reporters wonder whether Fieger understands that he can't create those fuzzy impressionist masterpieces for them as he does for a jury. As they listen to his latest tirades, they wonder vaguely when all of this will blow up in his face.

Or worse: What will he do when Kevorkian goes away?

On an early September Sunday, Fieger relaxes in his tasteful West Bloomfield Township home. It sits on a golf course, although Fieger doesn't play. The home is spotless, dominated by large, framed pieces of art, light colors and a baby grand piano, though Fieger doesn't play that either.

A cozy library reveals Fieger's leanings: "First In His Class," a book about President Bill Clinton; "The Lives of John Lennon"; "Wired," by Bob Woodward. There are Chekhov novels, books about Oscar Wilde, and volumes of plays. Foul-mouthed Fieger is a Shakespeare fan.

He wears a black, sleeveless T-shirt and black jeans, drinks spiked fruit juice, and pops vitamins. Keenie comes in with bagels. Kevorkian drops by and reads the newspaper.

Fieger and Keenie laugh over his picture on the front page of the Detroit News and Free Press, following another Kevorkian-assisted suicide. The camera caught Fieger with his hair flying in the wind.

"I look like I have wings," Fieger says.

"You look like Bozo," Keenie says.

During this weekend, he has done a session of "Good Morning America" and held two news conferences, plus radio shows and press interviews.

When all is said and done, the evidence will show that the Kevorkian case at some point took over Geoffrey Fieger's life. It has become his joy and his burden. It has brought him great reward, mostly in the way of recognition, since Kevorkian does not pay him.

But there have been costs.

Keenie, an architecture student, says the case has invaded their personal lives. They can't go anywhere without being recognized.

"I can't do bad things anymore," Fieger jokes.

People ask for autographs, interrupt their dinners, offer advice, criticize. Many weekends are consumed by interviews, the post-suicide calls, case preparation — or Fieger's preoccupation with the whole issue.

"It's his life," Keenie says. "It has evolved. It wasn't always that way. Even though Geoffrey does a lot of other cases, this takes every other moment."

He has no hobbies, she says. "He doesn't have time. All he does is work, so when it's time to relax, I think he's forgotten how."

Outside work, Fieger's personal life consists mostly of an early morning workout and an occasional show or dinner. Most days, he comes home exhausted, inconsolable if he has lost a case, and usually very quiet. He takes a couple of melatonin and falls asleep to CNN.

Fieger admits Kevorkian has taken time from Keenie. "I've got to learn to be more sensitive to her feelings," he says.

One wonders if he will have time. Each week seems to bring new twists, questions, insinuations. There is a growing public perception even among those who advocate assisted suicide that Kevorkian and Fieger have gone circus, that they are no longer the right messengers for the issue.

"That's wrong," Fieger says. "First of all, we're the only messengers. And second of all, the only circus is the police and the prosecutor. If we were priests and literally ascetic and not doing a thing, they would still accuse us of that because it's necessary since we're winning.

"What did we do? We simply refused to back down and we simply refused to shut up."

If a time bomb is ticking, Fieger doesn't hear it. The play is the thing. The debate over assisted suicide "needs to go to a different level," he says. "The fact of the matter is ... we have been successful, overwhelmingly, on this issue in winning the hearts and minds."

So, ladies and gentlemen of the jury, what say you about Geoffrey Fieger?

He stands charged with offensive behavior, trickery, blustery; accused of lying, misleading, grandstanding; labeled as an egotist. He is a hero to his clients and a winner in court, but also an attorney burdened by his own choosing with an odd client and an issue that strikes at our souls: death.

Is Geoffrey Fieger acting or sincere? Does he care about assisted suicide, or just the notoriety it brings him?

Your verdict doesn't seem to matter to Fieger. After all, he needs only to worry about the opinion of his famous client.

Kevorkian isn't crazy about his lawyer's flamboyance, his profanity, his insatiable appetite for publicity. But he likes the way Fieger thumbs his nose at the system. And he likes the way he wins.

"I always felt my career and everything was a failure. And it still may be," Kevorkian says. "But I feel successful now because of the freedom I have to do what I want to do. ... He's helped me do that."

— *Sheryl James*

WILFREDO LEE

AN ALLY: DR. REDING

This article appeared in the Free Press on July 31, 1996. At this point Jack Kevorkian had assisted in at least 33 suicides.

A psychiatrist who observed five of Dr. Jack Kevorkian's recent assisted suicides has moved around the country and Michigan for three decades, kicking up controversy wherever he landed.

Dr. Georges Reding, 71, introduced by Kevorkian at a Washington, D.C., news conference as his new partner, has held at least four jobs in Michigan since 1990. He currently is a part-time contract worker for the Jackson-Hillsdale Community Mental Health Board.

He has had at least six complaints filed against him for alleged negligence in the last five years, state medical license records show. None resulted in any action against his medical license.

Thomas Lindsay II, a state health services official, said six complaints in five years is above normal. "I wouldn't characterize the number of complaints as unusual, but it's a little more than what we normally see," Lindsay said.

Before Reding arrived in Michigan, he held positions in Belgium, Switzerland, upstate New York, western Pennsylvania, central New Jersey and northern Illinois.

He declined to comment for this report. At his home in Galesburg, between Kalamazoo and Battle Creek in southwestern Michigan, his wife, Kathleen, said, "He does not speak to reporters."

But Reding told a National Press Club gathering that he joined Kevorkian because he was "embarrassed by the cowardice of my profession." Reding's involvement with Kevorkian, beyond being present at the assisted suicides and signing one patient's death certificate, is unclear. His name first emerged after the May 6 death of Austin Bastable.

Four months after he was licensed to practice in Michigan in 1990, Reding joined Kalamazoo Community Mental Health, staying for a year, officials said. While there, he began a "mobile crisis intervention" program in which he would visit patients in psychiatric crisis at any time in their homes. The program created controversy because of what some viewed as his gruff manner.

He was involved in the controversial suicide of a Vietnam veteran who jumped to his death from an eighth-floor window of a residential hotel in Kalamazoo in 1991. Reding had treated him.

His department was accused of letting the man, Charles LaMarr, out of a psychiatric hospital too soon. Local mental officials defended LaMarr's treatment, noting the state's policy encouraging agencies to move mental patients from expensive hospital treatment into community housing.

Typical of many complaints that trailed Reding during his time in Kalamazoo was an April 30, 1991, letter signed by 15 mental health patients and advocates.

The letter to the Bureau of Health Services, then part of the Department of Licensing and Regulation, said some patients suffered mentally and physically under Reding because of his unorthodox methods.

"Dr. Reding has taken some clients totally off medications and told them they didn't have a mental illness; others he has thrown over the trunk of his car and shot full of neuroleptics. Most of the clients he has taken off medications became psychotic and had to be put back on medication," the letter said.

Reding worked for Calhoun Community Mental Health around 1992. In 1993, Reding signed a one-year contract with Ionia Community Mental Health Board, but left after a few months. Jane Phillips, contract manager for Ionia CMH, said records did not show why Reding left.

He was also at Three Rivers Area Hospital before beginning a two-year tenure at the Jackson-Hillsdale Community Mental Health Board about two years ago.

Bev Lewis, past president of the Alliance for the Mentally Ill of Michigan, said she began keeping a file on Reding after receiving complaints about him. AMI is an advocacy group made up of people whose relatives and friends are diagnosed with mental illnesses.

"He told one man with manic-depression that he needed a swift kick in the butt and should throw his lithium away," Lewis said.

The man did and lapsed into a disabling psychosis, she said. Reding refused to take the man back as a patient, Lewis said.

Lewis said others complained that Reding told patients they didn't need medication because they weren't mentally ill, or they didn't need to be admitted into a psychiatric hospital.

"He believed no one needs hospitalization. Ever. I can't even begin to tell you how much havoc he's caused," Lewis said. "... He never stays anywhere for long because there isn't any place he's been that will put up with his behavior."

Michigan has 52 CMH boards that treat the mentally ill. The boards are publicly funded and typically pay less than the private sector, making it more difficult to attract specialists such as psychiatrists. Why Reding jumped from one position to another is not clear.

Lewis said she filed a complaint against Reding and has written to the state Department of Mental Health.

Michael Schwartz, a Kevorkian attorney, on Tuesday brushed off the complaints and controversy that have followed Reding.

Anyone can file a complaint against a doctor, Schwartz said.

"If you are voicing your opinions, there will always be some who like you, and some who do not," he said.

Schwartz said he has met Reding several times and he believes the doctor is "very professional."

Throughout his career, Reding has met controversy head-on.

During a four-year tenure in tiny Malone, N.Y., Reding called a local doctor "a quack" and told another he should be restrained from practicing medicine.

"It wasn't a pleasant experience," recalled George Pond, a member of the Franklin County board of legislators that fired Reding in 1972 as county director of mental health.

"He was very able and competent, don't get me wrong. But the problem was his personality," Pond said. "He couldn't get along with people. He didn't have a very good bedside manner."

In the town of about 6,000, Reding, who was raised and trained in Belgium, found plenty of trouble, especially when he was determined to break new ground, former associates said.

"He was probably very ahead of his time and he was in a very volatile role," said Ellen Maroun, a therapist who worked as an office assistant to

Reding not long after he arrived in 1968.

"He strongly believed in family therapy, not just the individual, but everyone involved."

County officials saw Reding as a nuisance who paid little heed to anyone he viewed as inferior to himself, Pond said. "He condescended quite a bit," he said.

What angered Reding's bosses was a once-novel, now-common approach to psychiatric treatment — sending patients suffering from acute psychiatric emergencies to general hospitals instead of mental hospitals more than 60 miles away.

"People's comfort levels were challenged," Maroun said. "He was supportive of people working through their problems."

Ironically, some of the patients were on the brink of suicide.

"This is a very isolated county and that approach, I'm told, was difficult to stomach," said Claire Stratford, director of Northstar Mental Health Services, the agency that followed Reding's experiment.

Despite a huge rate of success, according to an article Reding cowrote for the New England Journal of Medicine, townspeople sent him packing, ostensibly for mismanaging his $200,000 budget as mental health director.

They complained about excessive mileage because he drove 25,000 miles a year within the county checking up on patients, according to published accounts of his departure.

"He says that only about one in five doctors cooperated with the psychiatric hospitalization project and the rest 'tolerated' it," said a Science magazine article detailing his work in Malone.

Maroun told the magazine that Reding's forced departure — the mental health board refused to fire him so legislators simply stopped his funding — was a "county-level Watergate."

Reding also left more than medical controversy in his past, Maroun said.

"He divorced his first wife, Lorna, and married a nun," she said.

Others in the town confirmed that Reding married Sister Kathleen, an Ursaline nun who helped in an alcoholic rehabilitation program.

From the New York mountains, Reding went to Coudersport, in a rural, poor county in western Pennsylvania where he plied his ideas of community mental health programs. He stayed two years before saying he had to leave so he could put his four children into good schools.

After stints in New Jersey, New York City and its suburbs, Reding came to Michigan in May 1990, records show.

— David Migoya, Chris Christoff and Wendy Wendland

MICHELLE GABEL

A DIFFERENT DR. DEATH

This article appeared in the Free Press on Dec. 16, 1996. At this point Jack Kevorkian had assisted in at least 45 suicides.

Once or twice a month, Dr. Tim Quill picks up the phone and finds on the line a stranger who wants to die.

They may have seen him on TV or read his books helping people find death. They may know about Diane, a leukemia patient for whom Quill prescribed the sleeping pills she used to end her life.

But their hopes are misplaced. Quill has admitted assisting two suicides, but he does not deliver death on demand.

"People who call for that kind of help, I refer them back to their own doctors. For me, this only makes sense in the context of a long-term relationship," he said in an interview. "I try to keep what I do pretty mainstream."

In contrast to Dr. Jack Kevorkian, Quill is calm, exudes respectability and is a practicing physician.

Kevorkian, the retired pathologist, has called Quill a fraud and a coward because Quill has not aggressively offered suicide assistance, nor was present when his patients died.

But as right-to-die advocates have grown in number and credibility, some say they have become increasingly uncomfortable with Kevorkian's actions, particularly his role in the suicides of three women who may not have been terminally ill.

With their cause taking center stage before the U.S. Supreme Court in a case that bears Quill's name, they are promoting the soft-spoken Rochester, N.Y., doctor as a more fitting symbol of the right to die.

"I don't mean to put Dr. Kevorkian down. I'm just saying that he's not the model. Quill is the model," said Faye Girsh, executive director of Hemlock Society USA, which lobbies for legalizing assisted suicide.

"If we had more doctors like Tim Quill, we wouldn't have a problem," she said recently. "Dr. Quill is the perfect doctor to have help you die."

Quill, 47, a professor of medicine and psychiatry at the University of Rochester and a primary-care internist who spends about half his time seeing patients, accepts the mantle reluctantly.

"I don't want to be a symbol of anything in particular," he said during an interview in his office deep inside the big, brick Genesee Hospital complex on the edge of downtown Rochester.

"I realize I've become probably the most vocal physician in talking about this, but I'm not really an advocate of assisted suicide. I'm an advocate of not abandoning people."

Quill stumbled into the assisted-suicide spotlight almost by accident when the New England Journal of Medicine published his article about Diane. A recovering alcoholic who had survived vaginal cancer, Diane developed acute leukemia. Quill has never identified her or said exactly when he treated her.

Offered a painful regimen of chemotherapy that carried a one-in-four chance of survival, Diane said no. As she deteriorated, she asked Quill to help her die. She took the pills in her living room, alone, to avoid exposing Quill or her family to prosecution.

Quill wrote about the case in 1991, months after Kevorkian had made his startling debut by helping Janet Adkins, 54, an Oregon woman with Alzheimer's disease, die in Michigan with a machine that gave her a lethal injection.

Quill said he believed the Adkins case sensationalized a legitimate point: It is sometimes appropriate for a doctor to help someone die.

Quill said he believed his experience with Diane would add credibility to the debate in professional circles. "I thought it would be hard to dismiss coming from me, because I have academic credentials and I'm an upstanding member of the medical community and all that stuff."

He said he underestimated the impact of the article, both with the public and the legal community.

As the first practicing physician to publicly describe his own role in a suicide, Quill made headlines across the nation — and drew the attention of local prosecutors. But he told his story to grand jurors, and they refused to indict him. Prosecutors were not surprised.

"Dr. Quill has a very good reputation in this community," said District Attorney Howard Relin of New York's Monroe County. "This was far different from the Kevorkian cases. It was clear to everyone here that Dr. Quill was not embarking on a crusade ... or looking for ways to embarrass law enforcement or to get publicity for himself."

After his "legal adventure," as Quill calls it, he did launch something of a crusade. But instead of dropping bodies on hospital doorsteps as Kevorkian has done, Quill challenged the New York law that bans assisted suicide.

He and two other doctors argued in the lawsuit against the state that a terminally ill patient who requests a lethal prescription is no different from a patient who exercises his legal right to refuse life-sustaining treatment. By making one request illegal, they argued, the law discriminates against terminally ill people who do not depend on life support.

The 2nd U.S. Circuit Court of Appeals agreed, striking down the New York ban.

The case neatly summarizes Quill's belief that writing a lethal prescription is morally and ethically equivalent to unplugging a respirator. The argument is more fully explored in Quill's book "A Midwife through the Dying Process" (The Johns Hopkins University Press, $24.95).

The book tells the stories of nine people who chose to end their lives while under Quill's care. AIDS victims, cancer patients, a young father struck by Lou Gehrig's disease — most battled valiantly before they chose to stop fighting.

A man identified only as Jules, an amyotrophic lateral sclerosis victim, set a date for his respirator to be turned off. He died immediately, with his family around him.

Another, identified as Mr. Kline, a cancer patient in extreme pain and terror, was sedated to unconsciousness at the request of his family, leaving him unable to eat or drink. He died after five days.

Mr. Williams, one of the more bizarre cases in the book, demanded that doctors deactivate a cardiac defibrillator implanted in his chest. The device had extended his life for years, but became horrible as Mr. Williams neared death, repeatedly shocking his failing heart back to life. With the apparatus turned off, Mr. Williams lasted three weeks.

All these decisions are legal examples of refusing or withdrawing treatment. But in Chapter 8, Quill comes to Jane.

Jane was his second assisted suicide. (He said there have been no others since then.) Relin, the prosecutor, blanched when he heard the story from a reporter. But with the New York law in limbo, he said another criminal investigation is unlikely.

Jane, a member of the Hemlock Society and a former smoker suffering from severe respiratory problems, asked Quill for sleeping pills soon after the grand jury ended its investigation into Diane's case.

"I was afraid you were going to ask me this," Quill responded to Jane, according to his book. His account continues: "Given my recent legal difficulties, I didn't feel that I could be physically present with her at the very end. ... I felt as if I were helping her and abandoning her in the same moment."

But he gave her the pills anyway. Six months later, Quill learned that Jane died in the company of two friends, who placed a plastic bag over her head when the pills seemed not to be working.

"I didn't like doing it. I definitely didn't want to get into another legal process," Quill said. "But you can't not come through for people. Shortness of breath was just terrifying for this lady. And she was getting worse and worse and worse."

Jane's condition did not fit the typical definition of terminal illness. Quill said he believes assisted suicide should be legalized only for the terminally ill, but he foresees a time when it would be made available to the chronically ill.

Opponents of assisted suicide say this is a step down the slippery slope. Such views, they say, make Quill no better than Kevorkian, whom they view as a serial killer.

"They both are accomplishing the same end, the one with a hacksaw, and the other with a fine surgeon's knife," said Dr. Michael McQuillen, a neurology professor at the University of Rochester.

"They're doing the same thing. It's just a question of the way you do your press releases and the way you select your patients," said Dr. Randolph Schiffer, a professor of psychiatry, neurology and environmental medicine who was chairman of a University of Rochester task force that looked at Diane's case and found Quill's actions improper.

Others see clear differences between Quill and Kevorkian.

"Kevorkian is like someone who comes to your home with a gun, shows you where to point it and how to pull the trigger," said George Annas, a medical ethicist at Boston University and a leading voice in the argument against legalization of assisted suicide. "Quill, on the other hand, he's a real physician. He's just doing good medicine — better than most."

"Quill's the guy you want when you're dying," Annas said. "Kevorkian's the one you want if you want to commit suicide."

Responding for Kevorkian, his lawyer, Geoffrey Fieger, told the Free Press that Quill "is a poster boy for some of the people that would have us talking about this for the next 4,000 years without doing anything about it."

Reminded that Quill has waged a legal battle on behalf of assisted suicide, Fieger said, "Yeah, he might be doing something about it, but meekly and sheepishly."

And Quill himself? He credits Kevorkian for bringing the debate into the open. But now the issue has entered the mainstream.

Kevorkian, Quill said, should step aside in favor of practicing physicians.

"He doesn't have the right skills," Quill said. "This debate is not about suicide. It's about what is good end-of-life care? And what do you do when that care doesn't work? Do you still have a responsibility? That's the core of the issue for me."

— *Lori Montgomery*

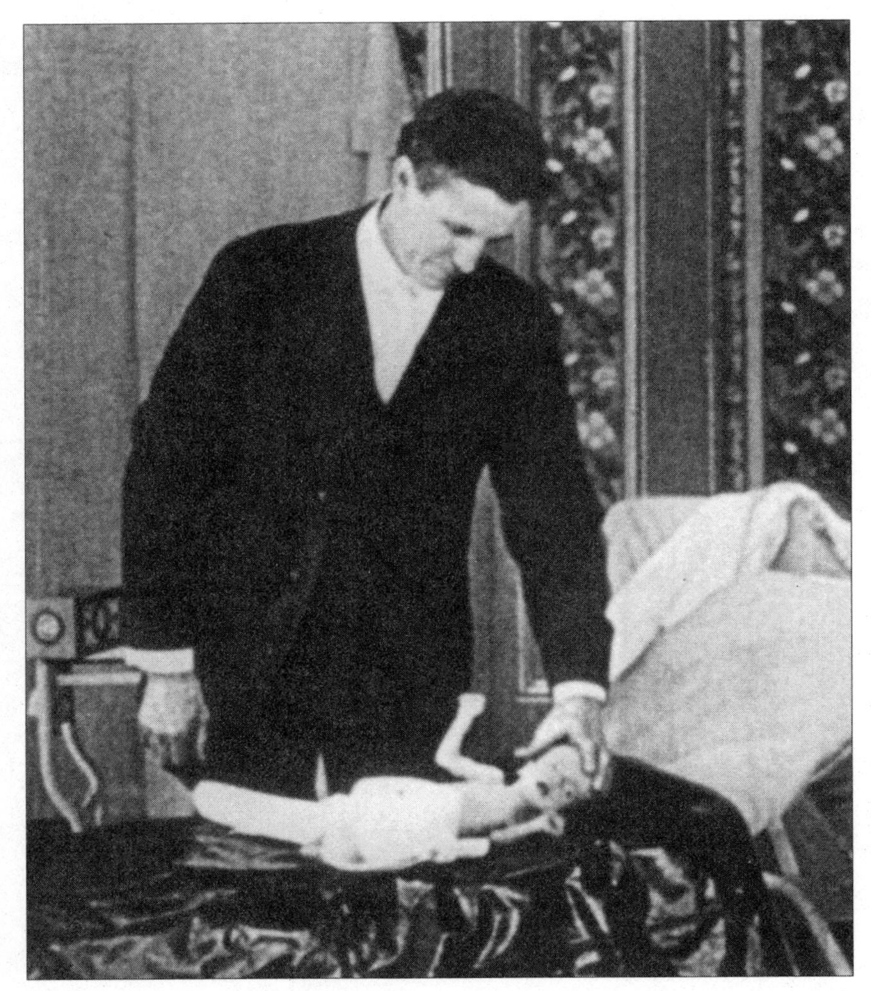

Dr. Harry Haiselden stands with the baby he refused to operate on in 1915, saying it was an act of kindness to let the deformed infant die. The baby's father and mother agreed.

PART FOUR

THE ASSISTED SUICIDE DEBATE

BLACK RELUCTANCE

This article appeared in the Free Press on Feb. 26, 1997. At this point Jack Kevorkian had assisted in at least 47 suicides.

The family came to the Rev. Jim Holley seeking guidance. Their elderly father was on a respirator. The doctors had said it was time to let him go.

The doctors seemed respectful. Still, the family wondered. Might the white doctors pull the plug on their black father to give the machine to someone else?

"True enough, when we went back in there, the man had passed. And the machine was being used by somebody else," Holley, the minister at Detroit's Little Rock Baptist Church, recalled recently.

A coincidence? Holley believes it was. But for many black families, he said, such a coincidence "does lend itself to suspicion."

From the notorious Tuskegee, Ala., syphilis study to more recent findings that black patients often get less treatment than whites, the black community has long seen evidence that the U.S. medical establishment devalues black lives.

Now, as the nation debates physician-assisted suicide and other limits on life-sustaining care, some black leaders fear right-to-die choices are giving doctors new opportunities to victimize blacks.

"There is a lot of suspicion," said University of Colorado research associate Annette Dula, one of a handful of black academics studying bioethical issues. "People know they don't get the health care they need while they're living. So what makes them think anything's going to be more sensitive when they're dying?"

The U.S. Supreme Court is expected to decide this spring whether doctors should be allowed to help people die. But assisted suicide is just one aspect of a much broader movement to improve care of the dying.

For many Americans, that trend is a blessing. But a growing body of research suggests that those who feel blessed are predominantly white.

Racial minorities, by contrast, are far less interested in having doctors help them die. Research shows they feel more threatened when health professionals talk to them about living wills. And black patients, in particular, are far more likely than whites to say they want aggressive treatment and life support no matter how sick they become.

There is no evidence to indicate these wishes are not honored. In fact, researchers say, the reverse is more often true — the wishes of dying people of all races who want to die without life support are often ignored.

But as the standard of care for the dying continues to evolve — and as cost looms ever larger as a factor in health care — some experts worry that black distrust of the medical establishment and its motives will be heightened.

"There are huge discrepancies in what people want," said Dr. Elizabeth McKinley, an ethics researcher at Case Western Reserve School of Medicine in Cleveland, who has studied black and white cancer patients.

"This is a very weird and different medical environment where everybody's bent out of shape over how much end-of-life care costs. It's being talked about all the time," McKinley said. "And if we start making policy decisions about terminating care, if we start saying you can't have things, I'm afraid people in the black community will become even more vulnerable and mistrustful."

Physician-assisted suicide is a flash point for this fear. Seven former and current members of the U.S. Commission on Civil Rights are among those who filed legal briefs before the Supreme Court arguing that the poor, the disabled and racial minorities would be the first to feel pressure to die if assisted suicide were legal.

The assisted-suicide cases before the high court are being closely watched by black leaders across the nation. And the outcome is keenly awaited in Detroit, where black leaders have had a front-row seat for the career of Dr. Jack Kevorkian, a retired West Bloomfield pathologist who since 1990 has helped 46 white people and one Hispanic die.

"Among more enlightened people, there is a sort of a paranoia in the back of our minds that, if assisted suicide becomes legal, then lawmakers will somehow find a way to manipulate the law ... to where African Americans are, to a greater extent than anybody else, receiving less medical care and are more often eliminated," said the Rev. James Perkins, minister at Detroit's Greater Christ Baptist Church.

Meanwhile, Holley's experience with the dying Detroit father illustrates the distrust that already attends some end-of-life decisions for black families.

Until the 1980s, unplugging a respirator was rarely an option for anyone. Then court cases involving Karen Ann Quinlan and Nancy Cruzan established patients' rights to refuse life-sustaining treatment. A growing hospice movement created options for people to forgo painful therapies that might save their lives. And in 1991, a new federal law required hospitals to inform patients upon admission about their right to sign a living will, which tells doctors what treatment they want at the end of life.

As a result, patients and their families now face more decisions about death and more frequently find doctors willing to say the situation is hopeless and treatment should stop.

"I've had African-American clients ask me pointedly: 'Is this because we're black?' " said Margaret Campbell, an advanced practice nurse who runs the hospice care program at Detroit Receiving Hospital.

"I have, of course, gone on to assure the family the reason we're recommending comfort care is because the person is at the end of life and further treatment would not produce a good outcome," Campbell said. "Establishing trust goes a long way toward assuaging those concerns."

To establish trust, Campbell, who is white, says she presents pictures, an X-ray or a brain scan: Here's a normal brain, all lit up with flowing blood and firing neurons. And here's the patient's brain, dead and dark.

Alfred Bolden favors cotton balls. As Michigan project director for the Minority Organ and Tissue Transplant Education Program, a federally funded effort to increase organ donations among minorities, Bolden often has to convince bereaved families to pull the plug and give up their loved one's lungs, kidneys or heart.

With the family watching, "you rub the cotton over the eyeball," said Bolden, who is black. "Even in the most unconscious individual, there's going to be a reaction." A brain-dead patient won't even flinch. "And it becomes very clear to them, 'Hey, he didn't lie to me.' "

But brain death is not the only reason to stop treatment. And some doctors fear they don't do a good job of explaining that to minority patients and their families.

Those concerns have spurred a growing body of research to help doctors talk to minority patients about dying. One particularly telling finding: In a 1988-89 University of North Carolina survey of 2,500 elderly patients, only 6 percent of white patients said it was more important to live long than to live well. But 25 percent of black patients felt a long life was more important.

What researchers haven't been able to determine is why black and white attitudes about dying are so different.

Some experts speculate that black patients are disinclined to refuse care which, historically, they may not have been offered. Others point to a deep spirituality in the black community and a belief that God alone should dictate the hour of death. There is also a strong belief in miracles.

"When you live with a survivor mentality, you have faith, you have hope operative," Holley said. "There's always hope that the person's going to get better."

The North Carolina researchers noted that suicide rates are much lower among elderly blacks than elderly whites. Perhaps, they wrote, historical and cultural differences make "the black population in the United States ... unusually familiar with and prepared to struggle against death."

In her study of 206 North Carolina cancer patients published last year, McKinley hypothesized that trust is the primary factor. Her study showed that her black subjects were just as likely as whites to say they trusted doctors, but she doubts her findings.

"I still think there's a lot of distrust," she said in an interview. "And I think there are very good reasons to distrust the medical system."

Among them, experts said:

■ The Tuskegee experiment, which ended in 1972. For 40 years, government researchers studied 412 poor black sharecroppers with syphilis, telling them they were being treated when, in fact, they were not. All but a handful of them are dead now.

■ More recent studies showing that black patients are less likely than white patients to receive such high-tech treatments as heart-bypass surgery, pacemaker implants and hip replacements.

■ Less than 5 percent of U.S. doctors are black.

As discussions about dying become a more frequent part of the doctor-patient relationship, it's clear, experts say, that somehow trust must be increased.

Mary Harris Evans, a San Francisco stockbroker with degrees in law and medicine, recalls how her father died of cancer in 1963 at a hospital outside Mobile, Ala. The white doctors said there was nothing they could do. Most of the time, she thinks, they told the truth.

"But in my mind, I have always wondered: 'How do I know those doctors gave him the best treatment he could get?' " In 1963, she said, "You couldn't press the issue in Alabama."

Today, Evans is one of two black members of the board of the Death with Dignity Education Center, a nonprofit California organization that advocates legalizing physician-assisted suicide.

Evans supports a patient's right to choose to die. Still, she worries about the consequences of legalization. And she does not discuss the subject with black friends unless they ask.

"There's a big fear of genocide in our community, whether it's right or wrong," Evans said. "People in the black community see death with dignity as just another way for them to be offed."

— *Lori Montgomery*

HOW PATIENTS CHOOSE

This article appeared in the Free Press on June 20, 1996, the day of Jack Kevorkian's 31st reported assisted suicide.

Ruth was dying — but not quickly enough to suit her.

Suffering from rheumatoid arthritis and a fatal lung condition that left her panting for breath, the 79-year-old Southfield resident had been given drugs to make her more comfortable. But the medication frightened her because it made her drift in and out of consciousness.

"What I really want is Kevorkian," the woman gasped to her doctor. "And if you could give me an injection right now, that would be fine."

John Finn, chief physician for Hospice of Michigan, works to ease the dying of more than 7,000 terminally ill patients each year. But Finn carries no suicide machine in his medical bag.

He instead made Ruth the promise he usually makes to dying patients — one that can be honored lawfully in Michigan and every other state: He would do whatever was necessary to control her symptoms.

"When you are ready," he told her — "when you're suffering to a point that is unrelievable and unacceptable, we'll bring you into the hospital and we'll give you morphine by IV."

The dosage required to make Ruth comfortable might well leave her comatose, he explained; in her weakened condition, she would likely die within a few days.

Finn had one request — that his patient first talk to her rabbi. After that, Ruth could summon Finn anytime for the transfer to the hospital.

Two days later, Finn looked at his watch and noted that Ruth had yet to call. "Obviously, she hasn't made up her mind," he said. "But she has that option."

Ruth, whose name has been changed here to protect her privacy, is among the fortunate few. As a hospice patient, she enjoys pain relief options and emotional support not extended to most hospital patients.

Hospice — a philosophy of care, not a place — gives up on cures to focus on pain relief, emotional support, and spiritual help for the dying and their families.

But the vast majority of terminally ill Americans never are referred to hospice. Like the dying in most developed countries, they suffer instead with fears of dying long, isolated, and unnecessarily painful deaths in high-tech hospitals where doctors ignore their wishes and subject them to unwanted and futile treatment. And unfortunately, these fears are very well founded.

In Michigan, the failure to meet the needs of terminally ill patients has fueled a rancorous debate over physician-assisted suicide. But Jack Kevorkian's extraordinary crusade is just one facet of a national, even worldwide upheaval over how we die.

The debate is acquiring added urgency as tens of millions of Americans born after World War II — baby boomers committed to individual choice and consumer rights — approach the prime dying years.

Theirs is the first generation to grow up with medical technologies that have changed the definition of death since they became widely utilized in the '60s.

As a result, they were the first to see grandparents — and now, parents — die prolonged, painful deaths.

For more than three decades, the boomers' quest for individual expression and self-determination has driven mass culture and public policy. Now the generation that gave us the sexual revolution, the women's movement and the consumer rights movement seems determined to have death its own way, too — and the doctors, lawmakers and judges are totally unprepared.

By the middle of the year 2025, the U.S. population will have increased 26 percent to 335 million, but the elderly population will have grown many times faster, according to the latest U.S. Census Bureau projections. The number of people 65 years old and over will have risen 83 percent to 62 million; more than a million of those will be older than 95.

"We're going to move into an era when a quarter of the population will be in the elderly age groups," says Peter Morrison, a demographer with the RAND Corp., a world-renowned think tank. This is roughly double the current percentage.

Annual deaths in America will soar from 2.3 million to more than three million in the same period, up nearly one-third and headed higher. With so much more of the population facing imminent death, providing for dying people will become a full-blown crisis — the dying crisis.

Already, Hospice of Michigan's Finn sees the fears and desires of the baby boomers reflected in the acquittals that Michigan juries have handed Dr. Jack Kevorkian each time he has been criminally charged in an assisted suicide.

The jurors aren't necessarily reflecting support for Kevorkian's brand of assisted suicide, Finn believes. "It's a major indictment of modern medicine," he says. "They're not happy with the state of affairs. They're looking at their own deaths and they want to have options available for them."

When is life not worth living — and who decides? Those questions have remained central to the euthanasia debate at least since Ancient Greece. The debate's most recent chapter began in 1975, when growing anxiety about prolonging comatose and terminal patients' lives crystalized in the case of Karen Ann Quinlan.

Quinlan, a 21-year-old New Jersey woman, was hospitalized after she stopped breathing and lapsed into a coma for no apparent reason at a party. When she had been comatose for 3½ months, her parents asked the hospital to remove the respirator that appeared to be keeping her alive. But doctors and hospital administrators resisted through six months of court battles until a judge ordered them to comply with the parents' wishes.

Even after she was weaned from the respirator, however, Quinlan remained alive in a coma for eight more years, sustained by tube feedings and antibiotics until she finally died at 31.

The Quinlan case was the most prominent of several court battles in which patients or their families fought for the right to end life-sustaining medical treatment.

The Quinlan case and its aftermath firmly entrenched the "right to die" in U.S. law and sparked at least three reform movements:

- The hospice movement strove to get terminally ill patients out of high-tech hospitals and into the care of workers trained to minimize pain and provide emotional and spiritual support.
- The "living will" and "advance directive" movement created ways for people to provide detailed instructions about the care they wanted as they died.
- Medical educators began training physicians to communicate with seriously ill patients and to ask about their patients' wishes regarding medical treatment as the end of life approached.

But 20 years after the reforms were initiated, little has changed.

Though hospice is widely considered a great success, it reaches only about 340,000 people a year — less than 15 percent of those who die in America, according to the National Hospice Organization in Washington, D.C.

Most patients never take the time to execute a proper advance directive or living will, and even the few who do often see their express wishes ignored.

The failure of all these attempts to reform medicine is laid out in one of the most important modern research studies on medical care for the dying.

The four-year, $30-million study, funded by the Robert Wood Johnson Foundation and completed late last year, looked at over 9,000 seriously ill patients in five major teaching hospitals through the country.

After two years, the study's authors concluded that doctors routinely subjected their terminally ill patients to pointless treatment, ignored patients' specific instructions regarding treatment, and allowed patients to die in pain.

While 31 percent of the patients expressed a desire not to be resuscitated if their hearts or breathing stopped, less than half of their doctors even knew that such requests had been made. The study also documented excessive time spent in intensive care just prior to death and excessive pain for half the patients in the last three days of life.

Hospice of Michigan's Finn says the study, known as the SUPPORT study "essentially gave medicine an F-minus in regards to care of the dying, pain management, autonomy, choices, the physician's communication with patients' families."

The real issue, he adds, "is that we need a different kind of physician. One that isn't so technically based. One that can share the patient's humanity."

And that, he adds, will take a long time.

Finn's call for a fundamental change in medical care for the dying enjoys broad support, including that of the Right to Life organization, which fiercely opposes euthanasia and assisted suicide.

"Medicine's whole mission," says Ed Rivet, chief lobbyist and spokesman for Right to Life of Michigan, "is so focused on curing and healing and 'we can fix you' that we still haven't begun to think about what is medicine's role when we can't fix you."

DEFINING TERMS

Euthanasia comes from two ancient Greek words meaning "good" and "death."

Over the last century or so, the term has been used to describe actions ranging from a patient refusing extraordinary medical treatment to an elderly man being gassed against his will.

Active euthanasia occurs when someone takes direct action to hasten a death.

Passive euthanasia occurs when a doctor hastens death by withholding or withdrawing medical treatment or nourishment.

Voluntary euthanasia is performed at the request of the person whose death is being caused.

Involuntary euthanasia occurs when death is hastened, actively or passively, without the consent of the person being killed.

— *Kirk Cheyfitz*

NEW ATTITUDES ABOUT DYING

This article appeared in the Free Press on Dec. 26, 1996. At this point Jack Kevorkian had assisted in at least 45 suicides.

At the dawn of the century, most people believed that God alone determined when they died, and for many the call came quite early in life. At century's close, most Americans are living well into old age — and increasingly they decide for themselves when it's time to go.

The national debate over legalizing physician-assisted suicide reflects this trend, as people demand ever more control over the way they die.

But assisted suicide is just a minuscule part of the picture. Every day, thousands of Americans make perfectly legal decisions to forgo treatment, withdraw life support and otherwise hasten death.

"When I started 10 years ago, it was like a crime to stop an IV line or tube feeding of a dying patient. It would literally have to go through the legal-affairs department at the hospital," said Dr. John Finn, medical director at Hospice of Michigan, the nation's largest nonprofit service caring for the terminally ill.

Today, such decisions are routine.

"There has been a major shift," Finn said. "People recognize that it's not euthanasia. It's just appropriate medical care when further treatment is futile."

Simply put, many people are no longer willing to try everything to cling to a life they no longer find worth living.

The "let me die" attitude marks a revolution in the way Americans view dying and doctors.

Twenty-five years ago, hospitals tried to resuscitate virtually everyone who died in their care. Then the parents of Karen Ann Quinlan waged a long legal battle for the right to remove their daughter from a respirator. And the parents of Nancy Cruzan fought for the right to end their daughter's artificial feeding. Today, all patients have the right to refuse or stop any treatment, even if this leads to death.

Cases such as Quinlan's and Cruzan's — young women left in a permanent vegetative state by sudden tragedy — are extremely rare. But the changing nature of death has created a vast constituency for the rights they won.

"Most of us will die slowly," said Dr. Joanne Lynn, director of the Center to Improve the Care of the Dying in Washington, D.C. "Dying is now a big piece of your life."

According to a 1996 report by the American Medical Association's Council on Scientific Affairs, virtually everyone who dies in a hospital — and that's nearly half the 2.3 million U.S. deaths in 1995 — refuses cardiopulmonary resuscitation to restart their hearts.

It's unclear how often patients make that choice directly. A study in LaCrosse, Wis., found patients make their own decisions about half the time. Only about 10 percent of hospice patients at Detroit Receiving Hospital are able to do so, hospice workers say.

But another 20 to 30 percent of Detroit Receiving patients leave explicit written or oral instructions, said advance practice nurse Margaret Campbell, who tracks the decisions. And family members rarely stop treatment without a gut-level certainty that their loved one would have wanted it, Campbell said.

"We don't have to put people on machines," Campbell said. "People have had experience with loved ones dying in the past. They know pretty much which things they want for themselves and which things they don't."

Right-to-die advocates argue that doctors still wield too much control over dying patients' treatment, which often is withdrawn simply because it was started inappropriately in the first place. There is confusion about what's legal, they say. And many people are ready to go long before they become dependent on life support.

"It's a fortunate person who has something to withdraw. And it's a very fortunate person who has a physician who foresees their need and will counsel them about what they can withdraw," said Barbara Coombs Lee, interim executive director of Compassion in Dying, a right-to-die group in Washington state that filed one of the two assisted-suicide cases before the Supreme Court.

But experts on end-of-life care say hospitals' willingness to withhold or withdraw treatment indicates doctors are getting the message. With better education and communication, they say, there would be no need for physician-assisted suicide.

"The vast majority of calls we get are largely people being kept alive on life support against their wishes or their presumed wishes," said Dr. Judith Ahronheim, deputy executive director of Choice in Dying, a patients' rights group in Manhattan that operates a national crisis hot line.

"The take-home message from Choice in Dying is that just 10 percent of our calls are about assisted suicide," she said, "but well over half are disputes about life support."

Lynn, of the Center to Improve the Care of the Dying, is on the board of the American Geriatrics Society and helped prepare a brief filed with the Supreme Court. The brief, which opposes legalizing assisted suicide, also describes a dramatic transformation over the past 100 years in the way people die.

At the turn of the century, the brief says, "dying afflicted every decade of adult life, nearly evenly." The most common causes were infection and accidents, which killed fast.

Today, the average person dies at 77. In 1995, nearly three-quarters of all U.S. deaths were people over 65.

The most common causes: Cancer, heart disease, dementia and other system failures. Death generally occurred, the brief says, after "progressive disability over more than a year."

Living with dying, Lynn said, is a "modern problem." It is not one that medicine knows much about.

"There really was a serious societal imbalance in 1950s, '60s and '70s. We thought if we worked at it hard enough, we'd conquer every disease," Lynn said. "In that context, a medical school dealing with dying was like a war college teaching soldiers how to surrender."

The crusade had successes as many diseases were vanquished and people lived longer. But it was almost too successful. People were horrified to see deteriorating relatives repeatedly revived and patched up, only to endure gruesome deaths with tubes in every orifice.

Such grim spectacles led to the Quinlan and Cruzan cases, to the creation of living wills, and finally to the assisted-suicide movement.

In one study, researchers at the National Institute on Aging examined the deaths of everyone 65 or older during 12 months in 1984 and 1985 in affluent Fairfield County, Conn.

The good news: Most spent their last year living at home. Virtually all spent time with family during their last three days. Half were able to recognize family and friends right up to the end.

The bad news: Most experienced a long slide into poor health, limited mobility and helplessness. Relatives said 35 percent were "aware they were dying" a month before they did.

The night before they died, about two-thirds were in the hospital or a nursing home. Only 35 percent spent their last night at home.

"Overall, we were encouraged by the fact that a majority of our sample was not alone and isolated at the time of death. And a majority were not in pain," said National Institute on Aging statistician Dwight Brock.

But there was "a significant decline in terms of the activities of daily living," Brock said. "Mobility. Hearing. Visual function."

And their medical conditions are unlikely to improve in the hospital, especially for the seriously ill. Various studies have shown that anywhere from 5 percent to 52 percent of terminally ill patients die in pain, according to the AMA council report. About a quarter experience the terrifying feeling of suffocation.

Doctors — who have not been trained to treat the symptoms of dying — may not adequately medicate these patients for pain, experts say. Yet, they are likely to order treatments that extend life.

A study to be published next month in the Annals of Internal Medicine looked at more than 3,300 seriously ill or very old patients who died in five large teaching hospitals. Relatives said 60 percent would have preferred comfort care to relieve symptoms. But 56 percent received life-sustaining treatment — a feeding tube, a respirator or CPR — in their final days.

Fortunately, hospice programs, which specialize in providing comfort to dying patients, are growing. The National Hospice Organization estimates that its members care for one in every seven people who die nationally, usually after they and their relatives have decided to stop seeking a cure. The average stay in a hospice is just three weeks.

Detroit Receiving Hospital's hospice service is one of the nation's oldest hospital-based programs. Campbell, who runs the service, said 70 percent of patients who come to her on respirators die after a deliberate decision to withdraw.

Ten years ago, only about 10 percent of her patients' respirators were deliberately unplugged. What's changed?

"It may be our own confidence with discussing withdrawal as an option," Campbell said. "But also, the lay public has become real pragmatic. As far as many patients are concerned, if he's not going to get better, what's the point?"

— *Lori Montgomery*

Starving as a Legal Option

This article appeared in the Free Press on Nov. 20, 1996. At this point Jack Kevorkian had assisted in at least 45 suicides.

First, there was Dr. Jack Kevorkian's death machine. Then the plastic bag became the symbol of the right-to-die movement. Now, another weapon has emerged in the arsenal of mercy: Starving to death.

At a time when the U.S. Supreme Court is studying the legality of physician-assisted suicide, voluntary starvation and dehydration are gaining support as an effective, legal alternative. Advocated primarily by a small but growing number of leaders in the hospice movement, refusing food and water is an option desperate people can exercise now, without a court ruling and without a prescription.

Experts at a forum on end-of-life issues in New York City said they see few legal barriers to the method. Patients have won the right to refuse treatment, including nutrition. And doctors may legally offer painkillers and other comfort as these patients die.

"Every single piece of the recipe is legal. And no lawyer has explained why putting them together as a package would be illegal," Howard Brody said in a telephone interview from Michigan State University, where he is director of the Center for Ethics and Humanities. "If doctors are morally OK with the idea ... I think it should be offered."

There are drawbacks: Caregivers opposed to physician-assisted suicide may see little difference between giving people a lethal dose of drugs and making them comfortable while they starve. And some find the notion of doctors telling patients to stop eating and drinking rather chilling.

Then there's the issue of time. Compared to taking a handful of pills, starvation is not quick. Death typically comes in one to two weeks.

"Why take 10 days when you can take 10 minutes?" said Faye Girsh, executive director of Hemlock Society USA. "I mean, what's the point?"

Ed Rivet, legislative director for Right to Life of Michigan, agreed that refusing food and water is "clearly within the law." But "to many people, it's probably not going to be a real appealing option. How do you dress up starving to death?"

More hospice workers and bioethicists, however, are spreading the word that refusing food and water is typically not painful for terminally ill patients. In fact, research shows that starvation may produce just the kind of gentle, peaceful passing that so many people say they seek.

"I would like to see us promoting this as a better and more autonomous option" to lethal prescriptions, said Connie Holden, executive director of Hospice of Boulder County, Colo., a home-care program that serves about 375 people a year.

"I've been around a lot of people who have chosen it and it's not painful. The main thing people have is thirst. But you can counter that with ice chips."

During the Hemlock Society's annual convention in Denver, Holden put on a skit depicting the advantages of dying by starvation. Earlier, she pressed the issue in a speech before a meeting of the Visiting Nurses Association.

She is also urging her hospice's ethics committee to adopt guidelines that permit information about voluntary starvation and dehydration to be given to patients. And, as a member of its ethics committee, Holden hopes to present the issue to the National Hospice Organization soon.

"The Hemlock people groan when you say this takes a couple of weeks," Holden said. "But that might not be any slower than trying to find a doctor" who will help a patient who wants to die.

Though skeptical, Girsh devoted two pages to the issue in the current Hemlock newsletter, writing that "I would endorse this as a legitimate alternative to which our members should give careful consideration, particularly when other means are not available."

Patient refusal of nutrition and hydration — PRNH, as it's referred to in the medical journals — is nothing new. Centuries ago, elderly members of American Indian tribes wandered into the woods to die without food or drink. Today, many terminally ill people stop eating and drinking simply because they are very sick and have no appetites.

What's new is the notion that refusing food and water could be an alternative to doctor intervention in hastening death — and that medical caregivers should recommend it to a suffering patient.

That idea emerged in medical journals in the late 1980s, and gained a wider audience in 1994, when the Journal of the American Medical Association published "A Conversation with My Mother."

The article was written by David Eddy, a health care researcher who lives in Washington, D.C. It described the death of his mother, Virginia Eddy, a "proverbial little old lady in sneakers" who had led a happy and independent widowhood in picturesque Middlebury, Vt. But surgery to correct a painful rectal condition left her "totally incontinent ... bedridden, anemic, exhausted, achy and itchy," her son wrote. When failing eyesight left her unable to read at age 84, she asked her son to help her die.

They considered drugs, an illegal route that made David Eddy nervous. Virginia Eddy also was put off by the idea of putting a plastic bag over her head to guarantee suffocation if she fell asleep before taking the full dose. This, she thought, would make a terribly depressing picture.

Hospitalized for pneumonia, she signed a do-not-resuscitate order and asked her son: "What else can I do?" And it dawned on David Eddy that his mother should stop eating and drinking.

It took just six days.

On her 85th birthday, she savored a last piece of chocolate and settled in to wait. Under her doctor's care, she cheerfully spent four days reminiscing, sleeping often but waking "brightly." On the fifth day, she was still smiling, but too weak to talk. On the sixth day, she didn't wake at all.

"Without hoarding pills, without making me a criminal, without putting a bag over her head and without huddling in a van with a carbon monoxide machine, she had found a way to bring her life gracefully to a close," David Eddy wrote. "Because she was happy, we were happy."

Since the article appeared, more than 100 people have contacted David Eddy about replicating his mother's death.

"It was such an obvious thing," Eddy, 55, said in an interview. "My knowledge of this was not much more than the average intelligent person. But I knew that if you're in the desert, you're not going to last very long. And the important thing is water, not food."

Eddy's only concern, he said, was that his mother's "pleasant" death was somehow "unusual and that I might be misleading people." But a growing body of evidence supports the assertion that Virginia Eddy's experience is common among patients who refuse food and water.

"Virtually any patient with far-advanced illness can be assured of dying — comfortably, without any additional distress — within one or two weeks simply by refusing to eat or drink," according to Ira Byock, a Missoula, Mont., specialist in end-of-life care writing last year in the American Journal of Hospice & Palliative Care.

This is true for a variety of reasons: First, terminally ill patients naturally lose their appetite for food and water. Indeed, caregivers often find it difficult to help a sick person maintain a healthy intake of calories and fluids.

When patients stop eating, they may feel hungry, but the sensation lasts less than 24 hours. At that point, a chemical process called "ketonemia" occurs, suppressing hunger and producing a mild euphoria.

When patients quit drinking, they are likely to feel thirst and develop dry mouth. But they can be kept comfortable with hard candy, oral swabs and balms, ice chips and sips of water. Meanwhile, the absence of liquid may reduce suffering by easing swelling, bloating and fluid collection in the lungs, which produces the terrifying feeling of suffocation.

In a 1995 study of 32 hospice patients who chose to stop eating and drinking, one-third said they never felt hungry or thirsty. Another third said they felt hunger, but that it quickly subsided.

Two-thirds felt thirsty, with 38 percent saying thirst plagued them throughout their final days. But all 32 patients reported relief through oral care and small sips of fluids.

In the end, research shows, the dehydrated patient's organs fail — particularly the kidneys and the heart. Doctors report dizziness, confusion and a "deepening somnolence with the person often described as having 'slipped away,' " Byock wrote.

In a 1990 survey of hospice workers, 86 percent of doctors and 89 percent of nurses found refusal of food and water to produce "peaceful comfortable deaths" in their terminal patients.

Though Girsh, of the Hemlock Society, finds this research persuasive, she is troubled by one case, in which a 78-year-old woman survived 42 days without food and 29 days without fluids. The woman reported no pain at all, but Girsh found the case horrifying.

"If prisoners on Death Row were sentenced to die this way, the ACLU would file suit so fast it would make your head spin," Girsh said. "I can't understand why it's the only method that's being blessed by everybody."

But Byock, president-elect of the American Academy of Hospice & Palliative Care, sees obvious benefits. He opposes efforts to legalize doctor-assisted suicide because it would give physicians too much power, he said. Patient refusal of food and water, however, is already legal — and places control in the hands of the dying.

"I don't think it should be something we hand out at hospice admission, or even that it should be our first response to the person who asks," Byock said in an interview. "That's too quick, and it can convey the message that, 'Well, yeah, we think you're hopeless, too.' "

But "this is a way of satisfying the person who has a strong desire to control the timing of their demise," he said. As the national debate over doctor-assisted suicide intensifies, such requests, he said, are becoming far more common.

"I don't bring up this issue," Byock said. "But if they're persistent in wanting a lethal prescription, I help them notice that they don't need my permission to die."

— *Lori Montgomery*

IN FAVOR

Since Dr. Jack Kevorkian began helping people die in 1990, opinion polls have consistently shown majority support for the concept of physician-assisted suicide, with men more favorable to it than women. Results of a 1997 survey of Michigan voters:

Do you favor or oppose the idea of allowing physician-assisted suicide for people who are physically suffering, or terminally ill, but mentally competent to request help in dying?

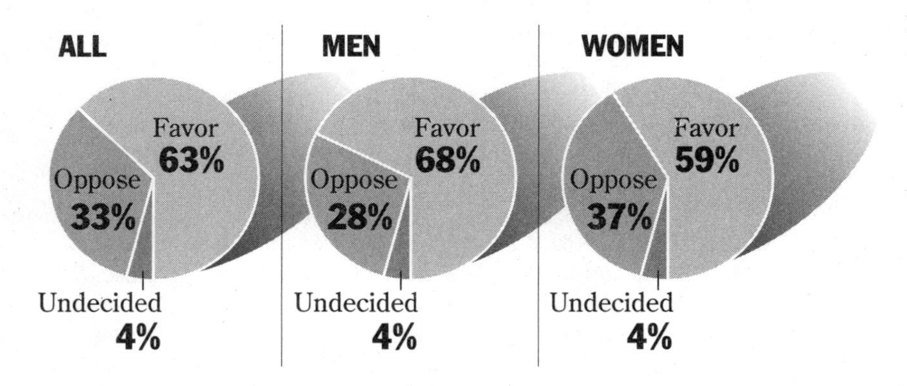

Source: Jan. 15-20, 1997, telephone survey of 600 Michigan voters by EPIC/MRA, Lansing. Margin of error for entire survey is plus or minus 4 percentage points.

DRAWING THE LINE

The 47 people believed to have died with Dr. Jack Kevorkian's assistance had a variety of reasons for deciding to end their lives. Often, it was a combination of things — pain, fear, weariness, a diagnosis that death was near or that continued deterioration was inevitable, depression, and feelings of indignity and helplessness.

Some cited their loss of independence due to illness and indicated a desire to take control of their deaths even as they were losing control of their lives.

About half the 600 people in the Free Press poll said they would consider physician-assisted suicide for themselves. The Free Press asked, "Where would you draw the line?"

Would these conditions cause you to consider physician-assisted suicide?

	Yes	No	Undecided
Need for life-support machines	**89%**	**5%**	**6%**
Chronic pain	**60%**	**26%**	**14%**
Loss of mobility	**50%**	**36%**	**14%**
Becoming a burden	**49%**	**40%**	**11%**
Loss of independence	**48%**	**38%**	**14%**
Less than 6 months to live	**43%**	**44%**	**13%**
Incontinence	**27%**	**63%**	**10%**
Prospect of nursing home	**25%**	**64%**	**11%**

AFTER KEVORKIAN?

One of the women aided in death by Kevorkian called him only after being assured by her minister that her decision would not exclude her from heaven.

Most respondents in the Free Press poll said they believe in the concept of heaven, and — contrary to some religious teaching — don't believe suicide keeps you out.

When life ends, some people will go to heaven if they lived a good life.

Agree	Disagree	Undecided/ don't know
65%	**20%**	**15%**

People who choose assisted suicide will not go to heaven.

Agree	Disagree	Undecided/ don't know
18%	**59%**	**23%**

DR. DEATH, 1915

This article appeared in the Free Press on June 20, 1996, the day of Jack Kevorkian's 31st reported assisted suicide.

The patient's death was just what the doctor ordered. He was so certain it was the right decision he invited reporters to join the death watch.

Alive, the helpless patient was a "burden to society" and himself, the doctor explained. Faced with a life of pain, misery and diminished mental capacity — a life not worth living — he was better off dead.

When the patient compliantly expired at 10 p.m. the next evening, his death made front-page news around the country.

The story sounds very modern and familiar. But this thin, death-dispensing doctor was not Jack Kevorkian.

This was 1915, in Chicago's German-American Hospital, and the physician was the chief surgeon and hospital president, Harry Haiselden.

There are significant differences between Haiselden and Kevorkian. But the similarities are striking, notes Martin Pernick, a University of Michigan history professor whose book, "The Black Stork," recounts Haiselden's story.

Kevorkian has limited his practice to adults who want to die. Yet the broad questions raised by Haiselden's long-ago campaign to euthanatize deformed infants are the same ones raised by Kevorkian's crusade:

Which lives are not worth living? And who will decide?

A look at the last 3,000 years of the euthanasia debate shows that not much has changed. The same ideas — the humanitarian goal of relieving the suffering of terminal patients and their families and the utopian impulse to improve society — have been intertwined at least since the ancient Greeks.

Euthanasia was extremely common in ancient times. The Old Testament book of Leviticus documents the ritual killing of infants in ancient Egypt and forbids it. The book of Genesis appears to tell a common story of how people reacted to hard times when it depicts the abandonment of a baby boy whose mother, Abraham's slave Hagar, could not find water for him to drink.

Some 400 years before Christ, Plato, the most influential of the ancient Greek philosophers, argued that physicians should refuse to treat chronically ill people who couldn't work. Anyone so afflicted, Plato wrote in "The Republic," had a "life not worth living."

Plato praised a physician who always withheld treatment from such patients, noting "he would not try ... to prolong a miserable existence and let his patient beget children who would likely be as sickly as himself." Thus the doctor's refusal to treat the patient not only helped end the patient's "useless" life, it also stopped the spread of "bad" human traits.

Hippocrates, Plato's approximate contemporary, known as the father of medical ethics, prohibited doctors from giving their patients deadly medicine, even if they asked for it. But he also wrote that physicians should not "treat those who are overmastered by their diseases, realizing that in such cases medicine is powerless."

In the Middle Ages, though, more and more Western physicians recognized a responsibility to alleviate the pain and suffering of dying patients. Gerrit Kimsma, a physician and philosopher at the Free University in Amsterdam, describes the development of the "sleeping sponge, as they called it ... in which various kinds of drugs were used to sedate a dying person." By the late 18th Century, medical ethics formally acknowledged a doctor's duty not to abandon his dying patient even when no cure is possible.

It is revealing that the modern history of euthanasia, particularly in the United States, is not so well documented.

Felix Adler, a prominent educator and scholar, was the first prominent American to call for laws allowing physicians to prescribe lethal drugs to suffering, terminally ill patients, according to Stephen Kuepper's unpublished doctoral dissertation, the only reliable, general history of euthanasia in this country.

Adler proposed a six-member commission of judges and doctors "to prevent abuses." Their job, recounts Kuepper, would be to grant death only if they could "unanimously agree on the hopeless condition of any patient requesting to die."

In 1906, the Ohio Legislature became the first to consider legislation to permit physicians to end the lives of terminally ill or mortally injured people who were requesting death. The bill never made it out of committee, but its introduction generated more publicity for the idea.

The broad public debate in America centered on similar calls for voluntary euthanasia — proposals to allow rational adults, suffering and near death, to request medical help to end their lives. But arguments simultaneously were being advanced for involuntary euthanasia.

In 1900, W. Duncan McKim, a New York physician, proposed a "gentle, painless death" for people with severe inherited defects. In a book titled

"Heredity and Human Progress," McKim suggested that candidates for death by carbonic gas would include the retarded, most epileptics, some habitual drunks, and numerous criminals — all then believed to be carriers of hereditary defects.

It would be a short 15 years until Henry Haiselden's bold, public campaign vaulted euthanasia and eugenics from the realm of academic debate to the black-and-white reality of death and the front page.

Anna Bollinger delivered her fourth child, a baby boy, in the German-American Hospital's maternity ward at 4 a.m. on Nov. 12, 1915. The attending physician saw immediately that the baby was badly deformed and not breathing well. Informed of the baby's condition, the father, Allen, said, "Don't let it live."

His wife agreed, and the hospital's chief surgeon, Dr. Haiselden, was summoned.

When Haiselden arrived, he found an infant partially paralyzed, missing its right ear and neck, its chest partially caved in, and no anal opening. The last condition would be fatal, Haiselden knew, unless he performed a simple operation to create an artificial opening.

Baby Bollinger was 4 days old when Haiselden called a news conference to announce he was refusing to operate and save the baby's life. As historian Stephen Kuepper describes the scene, "He explained that he would not kill the infant, but would 'merely stand by passively and ... let nature complete its bungled job.' "

Haiselden explained he was performing an act of "kindness" to save the baby from a life of misery in a wretched state institution.

But Haiselden also was a dedicated believer in eugenics — the then-popular theory that many bad human traits were hereditary and could be eliminated through selective breeding, compulsory sterilization of "defective" adults, and euthanasia.

Besides saving Baby Bollinger from a life of misery, he told the assembled reporters, he was sparing society from a mental defective who would likely grow into a criminal if he were allowed to live.

The Bollinger case became one of the most highly publicized in the history of modern medicine, and over the next three years, Haiselden withheld treatment from or killed at least five more abnormal babies, calling news conferences each time.

Pernick says a surprising number of prominent people supported the doctor, but his actions did not meet with universal approval. Many doctors, social workers, lawyers and judges condemned him. Some called him a murderer, and Illinois' attorney general demanded his prosecution.

But the local prosecutor refused to seek an indictment, and Haiselden's crusade won editorial support from the Detroit Free Press, the Detroit News, and other major newspapers across the country.

Haiselden promoted his euthanasia ideas to a mass audience through newsreels and newspaper stories, some of which he wrote. He even cowrote and starred in a feature-length silent movie, "The Black Stork," a thinly disguised dramatization of the Bollinger case that played in theaters for more than a quarter-century.

"Kill defectives, save the nations, and see 'The Black Stork,' a 1917 ad for the movie urged.

Invoking the same reasoning cited by Jack Kevorkian, Haiselden insisted his intent was to relieve suffering — his patients' deaths were an unintentional side effect. As Kevorkian would later maintain in court, Haiselden said he should be judged by his intentions, not the regrettable consequences.

This reasoning and the marriage of eugenics and euthanasia found horrifying expression in Nazi Germany. Between 1939 and 1941, in a program code-named T4, some 100,000 mentally disturbed, retarded, elderly and disabled Germans were given what Adolf Hitler described in a memo as a "mercy death" in showers that spewed deadly carbon monoxide gas.

When the techniques perfected in the mercy killings were turned on other groups — Jews, gypsies, and homosexuals — the resulting holocaust killed millions.

"Haiselden's anticipation of themes central to Nazi ideology does not make him the ... moral equivalent of a Nazi," writes historian Pernick. "But if Haiselden's ideas did not cause the Holocaust, both grew in similar soil."

The Holocaust is an enduring reminder of the evil extremes to which eugenics and euthanasia may be pursued. But in the 1970s, when doctors again began discussing withholding treatment from deformed newborns and comatose adults, the United States had contracted a case of near-total amnesia regarding Harry Haiselden.

Pernick, an expert in the history of medicine, medical ethics, and mass culture, is intrigued and concerned by our collective forgetfulness. "It's pretty clear that physicians have been practicing euthanasia for centuries," he said in an interview. "But public awareness is very cyclical. Each time the issue is rediscovered, the previous history has been forgotten."

Now, euthanasia is back in the news. Once again, it has been propelled to the front pages by a publicity-seeking doctor using shock tactics to get the attention of the news media. This time the form of euthanasia being promoted is called physician-assisted suicide. Once again, the practice is being widely advocated and passionately denounced. Once again, euthanasia is being practiced in the United States despite laws forbidding it.

This generation's Harry Haiselden is retired pathologist Jack Kevorkian, who has used lethal drugs and carbon monoxide to help 30 people kill themselves in the last six years.

And like Haiselden, Kevorkian has advocated euthanasia of a variety of people, including condemned prisoners. The potential benefits to society, Kevorkian has said, include more organ harvesting for transplants and more experimentation.

"I think individuals like Dr. Kevorkian do have a great deal of ability to reshape the public agenda if they are willing to put themselves completely on the line," says Pernick. "It's a tactical decision ... a strategic decision. It's a way of bringing out otherwise quiet supporters and shifting the spectrum of debate."

Kevorkian has excelled in using the media to define the debate as a vote on physician-assisted suicide. But the real issue, many medical and legal experts argue, is how to make suicide and euthanasia unnecessary by providing dying people with the medical care and comfort they want and need.

"The issue's not about physicians and suicide," says Dr. John Finn, chief physician of Hospice of Michigan. "It's about how we die in this country. It's about what needs to be available and what is society doing and what do we want to offer people."

— *Kirk Cheyfitz*

THE CHRONOLOGY

1990

June 4 — Dr. Jack Kevorkian helps Janet Adkins, a 54-year-old Portland, Ore., woman suffering from Alzheimer's disease, kill herself with his intravenous drug apparatus.

June 8 — Oakland County Circuit Judge Alice Gilbert temporarily bars Kevorkian from using his machine to help others commit suicide.

Sept. 12 — Sen. Fred Dillingham, R-Fowlerville, and Rep. Nick Ciaramitaro, D-Roseville, introduce legislation making assisted suicide a felony in Michigan.

Dec. 3 — Kevorkian is charged with first-degree murder in Adkins' death in Oakland County.

Dec. 13 — Oakland County District Judge Gerald McNally dismisses charges against Kevorkian, ruling that Michigan has no law prohibiting assisted suicide.

1991

Feb. 5 — Judge Gilbert issues a permanent injunction that bars Kevorkian from "conducting any acts to help a patient commit suicide."

Oct. 23 — Marjorie Wantz and Sherry Miller die of lethal injection and carbon monoxide poisoning, respectively. Wantz, 58, of Sodus, Mich., suffered from chronic pelvic pain. Miller, 44, of Roseville had multiple sclerosis.

Nov. 20 — State Board of Medicine suspends Kevorkian's license.

Dec. 18 — Oakland County medical examiner L.J. Dragovic rules Miller and Wantz deaths were homicides.

Dec. 19 — Oakland County Prosecutor Richard Thompson announces he will present the case to a citizens grand jury.

1992

Feb. 5 — Grand jury charges Kevorkian with two counts of open murder in the deaths of Miller and Wantz.

Feb. 28 — Kevorkian is ordered to stand trial on murder charges in the deaths of Miller and Wantz.

May 15 — Susan Williams, 52, of Clawson, dies by carbon monoxide poisoning. She had multiple sclerosis.

July 21 — Oakland County Circuit Judge David Breck dismisses murder charges against Kevorkian in the deaths of Miller and Wantz. He echoes McNally in saying Michigan has no law against assisted suicide.

Sept. 26 — Lois Hawes, 52, of Warren, dies after placing a mask over her face and turning on a canister of carbon monoxide. She had terminal cancer.

Nov. 23 — Catherine Andreyev, 45, of Moon Township, Pa., dies in Kevorkian's presence by inhaling carbon monoxide gas. She had terminal cancer.

Nov. 24 — The Michigan House approves legislation temporarily banning assisted suicide.

Dec. 3 — The state Senate approves an assisted-suicide ban, sending the measure to Gov. John Engler for his signature.

Dec. 15 — Marguerite Tate, 70, of Auburn Hills and Marcella Lawrence, 67, of Clinton Township become the seventh and eighth women to die with Kevorkian's help. Both die by inhaling carbon monoxide.

Dec. 15 — Engler signs the temporary ban on assisted suicide into law about seven hours after the deaths of Tate and Lawrence. The law makes helping someone commit suicide a felony punishable by up to four years in prison and a $2,000 fine. The legislation takes effect March 30, 1993, and imposes a 15-month ban on assisted suicide while a commission studies the issue.

1993

Jan. 20 — Jack Miller, 53, of Huron Township becomes the ninth person — and the first man — to die with Kevorkian's help when he inhales carbon monoxide through a mask.

Feb. 4 — Stanley Ball, 82, of Leland and Mary Biernat, 74, of Crown Point, Ind., die in Ball's lakeside bungalow by inhaling carbon monoxide gas from tanks supplied by Kevorkian.

Feb. 8 — Elaine Goldbaum, 47, of Southfield, dies in her apartment by inhaling carbon monoxide supplied by Kevorkian.

Feb. 15 — Hugh Gale, 70, of Roseville, who suffered from emphysema and congestive heart disease, kills himself in Kevorkian's presence by inhaling carbon monoxide.

Feb. 18 — Jonathan Grenz, 44, of Costa Mesa, Calif., and Martha Ruwart, 40, of San Diego, both suffering from terminal cancer, die by inhaling carbon monoxide at Neal Nicol's Waterford Township home.

Feb. 25 — Spurred by the three assisted suicides the week before, the Michigan Legislature approves a bill that makes the assisted-suicide ban effective immediately. The ban goes into effect shortly after Engler signs the bill at 5 p.m.

Feb. 25 — Oakland and Macomb county prosecutors obtain a search warrant, based on a document a right-to-life advocate told them she found in the garbage of longtime Kevorkian associate Nicol after Gale's death. Macomb County Prosecutor Carl Marlinga and Oakland County Prosecutor Richard Thompson allege the record of Gale's death was altered to hide the fact that Gale twice asked that the mask be taken off his face. The prosecutors say the case is being investigated as a homicide.

April 27 — Macomb County prosecutors exonerate Kevorkian in Gale's death, saying testimony from witnesses corroborates Kevorkian's assertion

Gale wanted to kill himself.

April 27 — A California administrative law judge, acting on a request from the state medical board, suspends Kevorkian's license to practice medicine there.

May 16 — Kevorkian attends the suicide of Ronald Mansur, 54, of Birmingham, the first he has assisted since the legislative ban took effect. Mansur had cancer.

May 20 — Michigan's ban on assisted suicide is overturned on technical grounds in Wayne County Circuit Court. Judge Cynthia Stephens rules that the ban violated the state constitution's one-subject-per-bill rule because it also set up a commission to study death and dying.

June 22 — The Michigan Court of Appeals orders the assisted-suicide ban to remain in effect while it reviews an appeal of Stephens' ruling.

Aug. 4 — Thomas Hyde, 30, of Novi inhales carbon monoxide. He had Lou Gehrig's disease.

Aug. 17 — Kevorkian is charged in Wayne County with assisting Hyde's suicide.

Sept. 9 — 36th District Judge Willie Lipscomb Jr. orders Kevorkian to stand trial in Detroit Recorder's Court in Hyde's death. Kevorkian is freed on bond. That night, Donald O'Keefe, 73, of Redford Township inhales carbon monoxide. He had bone cancer.

Sept. 14 — Kevorkian is charged with assisting in O'Keefe's suicide. Prosecutors ask for $250,000 cash bond, but 17th District Judge Richard Manning sets it at $10,000 on condition that Kevorkian not assist in any suicides. Kevorkian posts bond and is freed.

Oct. 11 — 17th District Judge Karen Khalil orders Kevorkian to stand trial in Wayne County Circuit Court on a charge of assisting in O'Keefe's suicide. Kevorkian is freed while his $10,000 bond is continued.

Oct. 22 — Merian Frederick, 72, of Ann Arbor inhales carbon monoxide in a room across the hall from Kevorkian's apartment in Royal Oak. She had Lou Gehrig's disease.

Nov. 5 — Detroit Recorder's Court Judge Thomas Jackson changes Kevorkian's bond in the Hyde case from personal to $20,000, ruling he violated probation by allegedly helping O'Keefe die. Kevorkian refuses to pay the $2,000 required to obtain his freedom and is held in the Wayne County Jail, where he refuses solid food.

Nov. 8 — Kevorkian is released after Macomb County lawyer John DeMoss posts his bond, complaining that Kevorkian is mocking the criminal justice system.

Nov. 16 — Wayne County Circuit Judge Richard Kaufman orders Kevorkian to stand trial for O'Keefe's death, but says the trial date will be moot if he rules the assisted-suicide law is unconstitutional.

Nov. 22 — Dr. Ali Khalili, 61, of Oak Brook, Ill., inhales carbon monoxide in the same room as Frederick did. Khalili had bone cancer.

Nov. 30 — Kevorkian is arraigned on charges of assisting in Frederick's suicide. He is ordered held on a $50,000 cash bond in the Oakland County Jail, where he stages another hunger strike.

Dec. 14 — Kevorkian is ordered to stand trial in Oakland County Circuit Court in Frederick's death. Later that day, Judge Kaufman dismisses charges against Kevorkian in O'Keefe's death and formally strikes down Michigan's ban on assisted suicide, calling it "unconstitutionally overbroad."

Dec. 17 — Kevorkian is released from jail after his bond is lowered to $100 and posted by a supporter.

1994

Jan. 4 — Oakland County Prosecutor Thompson issues a warrant charging Kevorkian with assisted suicide in the death of Khalili.

Jan. 6 — Michigan Court of Appeals hears arguments on the constitutionality of assisted-suicide ban and three related suicide cases.

Jan. 27 — Oakland County Circuit Judge Jessica Cooper dismisses assisted-suicide charges against Kevorkian in the deaths of Frederick and Khalili.

Jan. 30 — Kevorkian begins a petition drive to have the assisted-suicide issue put before Michigan voters on the Nov. 8 ballot.

March 28 — Kevorkian vows to help Margaret Garrish, a woman suffering from arthritis, whom he has counseled for two years, die unless a doctor prescribes pain medication. This comes despite his promise not to assist in another suicide until the Court of Appeals releases its ruling.

April 19 — Jury selection begins in Kevorkian's assisted-suicide trial in the death of Hyde.

April 25 — A state Commission on Death and Dying says it cannot reach a single recommendation on the issue of assisted suicide and instead will offer guidelines to the Legislature.

May 2 — Kevorkian is acquitted of assisting a suicide in Hyde's death.

May 10 — Court of Appeals agrees assisted-suicide ban is invalid on technical grounds but orders murder charges reinstated in the deaths of Wantz and Miller.

June 6 — Michigan Supreme Court agrees to hear appeal of Court of Appeals findings.

July 11 — Kevorkian fails to get enough signatures to put the assisted-suicide issue on the Nov. 8 ballot.

Oct. 4 — State Supreme Court hears arguments in assisted-suicide case.

Nov. 26 — Garrish, 72, of Royal Oak dies of carbon monoxide poisoning. She was the woman Kevorkian promised in March to help die if doctors did not prescribe pain-relieving medication. Oakland County Medical Examiner Dragovic calls her death a homicide.

Dec. 13 — Michigan Supreme Court rules there is no right to assisted suicide and that the state's ban is constitutional. But it also says the trial court must re-examine issue of murder charges in deaths of Wantz and Miller.

1995

April 24 — U.S. Supreme Court refuses to hear appeals of Michigan Supreme Court ruling upholding assisted-suicide ban.

May 8 — Kevorkian attends the death of the Rev. John Evans, 78, at Evans' Royal Oak home. Evans had lung disease.

May 12 — Michigan Court of Appeals affirms Judge Gilbert's Feb. 5, 1991, injunctive order. Kevorkian assists suicide of Nicholas Loving, 27, of Phoenix, Ariz. He had Lou Gehrig's disease.

June 26 — Erika Garcellano, 60, of Kansas City, Mo., dies of carbon monoxide poisoning. She had Lou Gehrig's disease.

Aug. 21 — Esther Cohan, 46, of Skokie, Ill., dies after inhaling carbon monoxide. She had multiple sclerosis.

Nov. 8 — Patricia Cashman, 58, of San Marcos, Calif., dies after inhaling carbon monoxide and receiving a lethal injection. She had cancer.

1996

Jan. 29 — Linda Henslee, 48, of Beloit, Wis., dies after inhaling carbon monoxide. She had multiple sclerosis.

March 8 — Oakland County jury acquits Kevorkian of murder charges in the deaths of Khalili and Frederick.

April 26 — Michigan Supreme Court denies Kevorkian's application for leave to appeal Judge Gilbert's injunctive order.

May 6 — Austin Bastable, 53, of Windsor, Ontario, dies after inhaling carbon monoxide. He had multiple sclerosis.

May 14 — Oakland County jury acquits Kevorkian in the deaths of Wantz and Miller.

June 10 — Ruth Neuman, 69, of Columbus, N.J., dies after inhaling carbon monoxide and receiving a lethal injection. She had recently been placed in a nursing home after suffering a stroke. An autopsy confirmed a brain tumor and diabetes.

June 18 — Lona Jones, 58, of Chester, Va., dies after inhaling carbon monoxide and receiving a lethal injection. She had a brain tumor.

June 20 — Bette Lou Hamilton, 67, of Columbus, Ohio, dies after inhaling carbon monoxide and receiving a lethal injection. She had syringomyelia.

July 4 — Shirley Cline, 63, of Oceanside, Calif., dies after a lethal injection. She had bowel cancer.

July 9 — Rebecca Badger, 39, of Goleta, Calif., dies after a lethal injection. She was diagnosed with multiple sclerosis but an autopsy found no sign of the disease.

July 25 — Kevorkian files writ with the U.S. Supreme Court to appeal Judge Gilbert's injunctive order.

Aug. 6 — Elizabeth Mercz, 59, of Cincinnati dies after inhaling carbon monoxide and receiving a lethal injection. She had Lou Gehrig's disease.

Aug. 6 — David Gorcyca defeats incumbent Richard Thompson in the Republican primary for Oakland County prosecutor.

Aug. 15 — Judith Curren, 42, of Pembroke, Mass., dies after a lethal injection. She had chronic fatigue symdrome.

Aug. 20 — Louise Siebens, 76, of McKinney, Texas, dies after a lethal injection. She had Lou Gehrig's disease.

Aug. 22 — Pat DiGangi, 66, of Suffolk City, N.Y., and Patricia Smith, 40, of Lee's Summit, Mo., die after lethal injections. Both had multiple sclerosis.

Aug. 30 — Loretta Peabody, 54, of Ionia, dies. Coroner initially attributes her death to natural causes. She had multiple sclerosis.

Sept. 2 — Jack Leatherman, 73, of Knoxville, Tenn., dies after a lethal injection. He had been diagnosed in May with pancreatic cancer.

Sept. 6 — Bloomfield Township police interrupt a motel room meeting between Kevorkian and Isabel Correa, 60, of Fresno, Calif., who suffered from a painful spinal-cord condition. They seize equipment and videos that depict Kevorkian meeting with three other assisted-suicide candidates, including Peabody.

Sept. 7 — Correa dies of carbon monoxide poisoning.

Sept. 29 — Richard Faw, 71, of Wilson, N.C., dies of carbon monoxide poisoning. He suffered from colon cancer.

Oct. 10 — Wallace Spolar, 69, of Horizon City, Texas, dies of carbon monoxide poisoning. He had multiple sclerosis and a bad heart.

Oct. 15 — U.S. Supreme Court allows Judge Gilbert's injunctive order barring Kevorkian from assisting suicides to stand.

Oct. 17 — Nancy DeSoto, 55, of Lansing, Ill., dies of carbon monoxide poisoning. She had Lou Gehrig's disease.

Oct. 23 — Barbara Collins, 65, of North Falmouth, Mass., dies of lethal injection. She suffered from ovarian cancer.

Oct. 31 — Kevorkian and two associates are arraigned on new criminal charges stemming from their role in 10 assisted suicides this year.

Nov. 7 — Kevorkian and his associate Janet Good are arrested and arraigned in Ionia after a grand jury indicts them for assisting Peabody's suicide.

1997

Jan. 10 — Newly sworn-in Oakland County Prosecutor Gorcyca announces he is dismissing criminal charges against Kevorkian and abandoning efforts to enforce Judge Gilbert's injunction.

Jan. 20 — Ionia County police seize the videotape of Kevorkian meeting with Peabody that was taken by local police in the Sept. 6 raid of Correa's motel room.

Jan. 30 — Bloomfield Township judge refuses to return seized materials to Kevorkian, saying that's for an Ionia Court to decide.

Feb. 2 — Lisa Lansing, 42, of Florham Park, N.J., a medical malpractice attorney who complained for more than a decade of pain in her digestive system, dies from a lethal injection. The body of Elaine Day, 79, a retired law office employee from Newhall, Calif., is found in Kevorkian's van parked at the Oakland County Medical Examiner's office. At one time an avid golfer, dancer and swimmer, Day had been increasingly disabled by ALS.

DAVID P. GILKEY

Dr. Jack Kevorkian makes a point from the witness stand in Oakland County Circuit Court on March 2, 1996. The murder trial ended in acquittal for Kevorkian.

PART FIVE
EDITORIAL

A BETTER WAY AWAITS

The Free Press special report "The Suicide Machine" makes clear why the debate over — much less the practice of — physician-assisted suicide simply cannot be entrusted to Dr. Jack Kevorkian. If competent, suffering, terminally ill adults are to have the right to enlist the help of doctors in choosing the time and manner of their deaths, as we believe they should, that autonomy must be anchored in a firmer set of societal regulations than the ever-changing whims of Doctor Death.

The newspaper series documented in exhaustive detail Dr. Kevorkian's reckless and self-aggrandizing behavior, his lack of standards or accountability to anyone — including his clients and their families — and his penchant for making things up as he goes along. Yet he has plied his public trade for nearly seven years because the politicians, prosecutors and police who have sought to stop him lacked support among jurors, voters and other Michigan citizens (including physicians) who share a belief in Dr. Kevorkian's cause, even if they properly disdain his methods.

As the series reported, many of the 47 people whom Dr. Kevorkian helped end their lives — often in an abrupt and grotesquely undignified manner — turned to him in despair, after their own physicians failed to treat them properly or simply abandoned them. Defining suicide as the only available alternative to unendurable physical agony or emotional terror and isolation is a choice no one should feel compelled to make.

Any legalization of physician-assisted suicide must be accompanied, if not preceded, by such things as more aggressive pain management by doctors and broader use of hospice care and other means of comforting dying patients. Above all, Americans need to start talking about death with their loved ones as well as their doctors, long before questions of such drastic measures as suicide arise.

Such private dialogues can usefully proceed in tandem with a public debate, in Michigan and across the nation, over the permissible conditions for assisted suicide. Merian's Friends, a Michigan group that seeks to place an assisted-suicide referendum on next year's statewide ballot, proposes several appropriate guidelines: The option of hastening death with a doctor's aid must be limited to adults who have less than six months to live, as certified by both the patient's own physician and an appropriate specialist.

A psychiatrist must certify that the patient is not acting out of depression or mental illness. Patients must make the request voluntarily, free of external coercion. They must be adequately apprised of alternative care and palliative pain-relief treatments. And they must be given at least a week to change their minds. Such standards are open to discussion and possible revision, but they surely are clearer and more consistent — and more humane — than the elastic rules Dr. Kevorkian and his apologists have articulated.

Despite the apparent futility of such a gesture, some state and national politicians seek merely to enact bans on physician-assisted suicide. A better course would be to adapt and apply to assisted suicide the standard President Bill Clinton has set for abortion: that it should be "safe, legal and rare."

Assisted suicide ought to be, by definition, a last resort. As such, it must be carried out far more carefully and sensitively than Jack Kevorkian's circus of death ever has done. Those who seek to make it a legitimate medical and legal procedure need to establish — now — that it is far too important to relegate to a ghoulish stranger in the back of a rusted-out van.

— *The Free Press editorial board*